Ordnance Survey

STRE ||||||||||||||||||||||| S
G000108047

South
Essex

Contents

PHILIP'S

First colour edition published 1999

Ordnance Survey® and George Philip Ltd, a division of
Romsey Road Octopus Publishing Group Ltd
Maybush 2-4 Heron Quays
Southampton London
SO16 4GU E14 4JP

ISBN 0-540-07297-4 (pocket)

To the best of the Publishers' knowledge, the information in this
atlas was correct at the time of going to press. No responsibility
can be accepted for any errors or their consequences.

The representation in this atlas of a road, track or path is no
evidence of the existence of a right of way.

**The mapping between pages 1 and 180 (inclusive) in this
atlas is derived from Ordnance Survey® OSCAR® and
Land-Line® data and Landranger® mapping.**

Ordnance Survey, OSCAR, Land-line and Landranger are
registered trade marks of Ordnance Survey, the national
mapping agency of Great Britain.

Printed and bound in Spain by Cayfosa

Digital Data

The exceptionally high-quality mapping
found in this book is available as digital
data in TIFF format, which is easily
convertible to other bit-mapped (raster)
image formats. The data can be
provided as pages or, in some regions,
as larger extracts of up to 200 sq km.
The larger extracts can also be supplied
on paper.

The index is also available in digital form
as a standard database table. It con-
tains all the details found in the printed
index together with the National Grid
reference for the map square in which
each entry is named and feature codes
for places of interest in eight categories
such as education and health.

For further information and to discuss
your requirements, please contact the
Ordnance Survey Solutions Centre on
01703 792929.

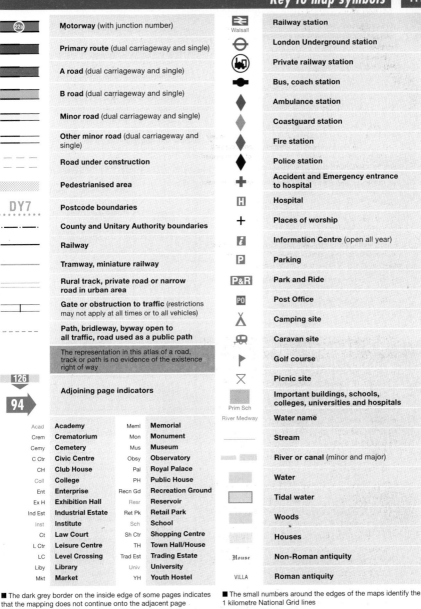

Motorway (with junction number)	Railway station
Primary route (dual carriageway and single)	London Underground station
A road (dual carriageway and single)	Private railway station
B road (dual carriageway and single)	Bus, coach station
Minor road (dual carriageway and single)	Ambulance station
Other minor road (dual carriageway and single)	Coastguard station
Road under construction	Fire station
Pedestrianised area	Police station
Postcode boundaries	Accident and Emergency entrance to hospital
County and Unitary Authority boundaries	Hospital
Railway	Places of worship
Tramway, miniature railway	Information Centre (open all year)
Rural track, private road or narrow road in urban area	Parking
Gate or obstruction to traffic (restrictions may not apply at all times or to all vehicles)	Park and Ride
Path, bridleway, byway open to all traffic, road used as a public path	Post Office
The representation in this atlas of a road, track or path is no evidence of the existence right of way	Camping site
	Caravan site
Adjoining page indicators	Golf course
	Picnic site
	Important buildings, schools, colleges, universities and hospitals
	Water name
	Stream
	River or canal (minor and major)
	Water
	Tidal water
	Woods
	Houses
	Non-Roman antiquity
	Roman antiquity

Acad	Academy	Meml	Memorial
Crem	Crematorium	Mon	Monument
Cemy	Cemetery	Mus	Museum
C Ctr	Civic Centre	Obsy	Observatory
CH	Club House	Pal	Royal Palace
Coll	College	PH	Public House
Ent	Enterprise	Recn Gd	Recreation Ground
Ex H	Exhibition Hall	Resr	Reservoir
Ind Est	Industrial Estate	Ret Pk	Retail Park
Inst	Institute	Sch	School
Ct	Law Court	Sh Ctr	Shopping Centre
L Ctr	Leisure Centre	TH	Town Hall/House
LC	Level Crossing	Trad Est	Trading Estate
Liby	Library	Univ	University
Mkt	Market	YH	Youth Hostel

DY7

126

94

Walsall

Prim Sch

River Medway

House

VILLA

■ The dark grey border on the inside edge of some pages indicates that the mapping does not continue onto the adjacent page

■ The small numbers around the edges of the maps identify the 1 kilometre National Grid lines

The scale of the maps is 3.92 cm to 1 km (2½ inches to 1 mile)

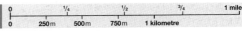

0	¼	½	¾	1 mile
0	250m 500m 750m	1 kilometre		

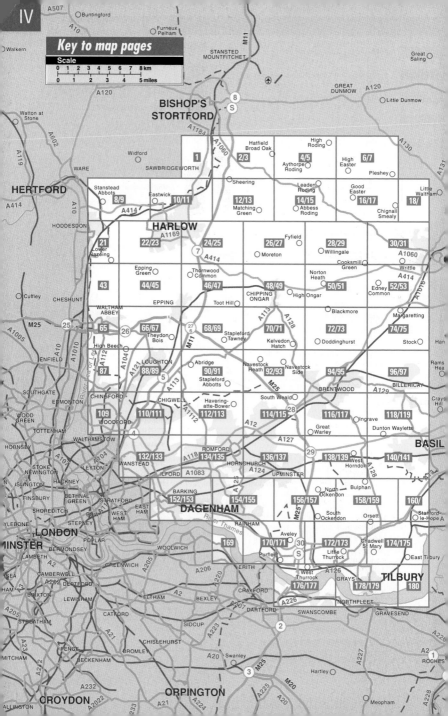

IV

Scale

0 1 2 3 4 5 6 7 8 km
0 1 2 3 4 5 miles

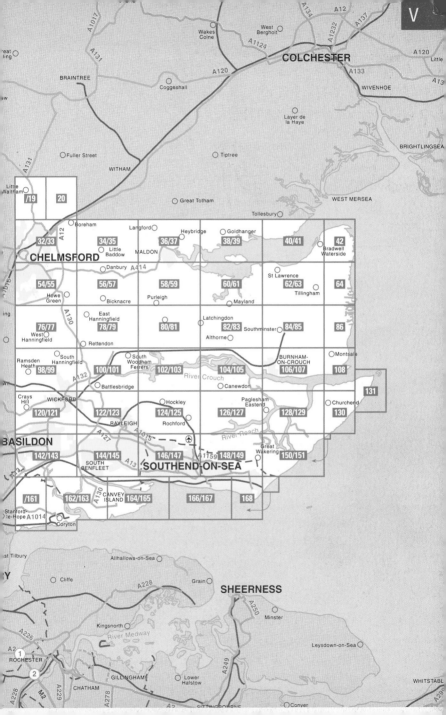

V

Great [...]ling
A1017
A131
BRAINTREE

Wakes Colne
A134
A12
A137
West Bergholt
A1124
COLCHESTER
A133
A120
A13[...]
Little
WIVENHOE
BRIGHTLINGSEA

Coggeshall
A120

Fuller Street
A131
WITHAM
A12

Tiptree

Layer de la Haye

WEST MERSEA

Little Waltham
/19
20

Boreham
32/33
A12
CHELMSFORD
Langford
Heybridge
34/35
Little Baddow
MALDON
36/37
Goldhanger
38/39
Tollesbury
40/41
42
Bradwell Waterside

Danbury A414
54/55
Howe Green
56/57
Bicknacre
Purleigh
58/59
60/61
Mayland
St Lawrence
62/63
Tillingham
64

West Hanningfield
76/77
East Hanningfield
78/79
Rettendon
80/81
Latchingdon
82/83
Althorne
Southminster
84/85
86

Ramsden Heath
98/99
South Hanningfield
100/101
South Woodham Ferrers
Battlesbridge
102/103
River Crouch
Canewdon
104/105
Paglesham Eastend
106/107
BURNHAM-ON-CROUCH
Montsale
108
131

Crays Hill
120/121
WICKFORD
122/123
RAYLEIGH
Hockley
124/125
Rochford
126/127
128/129
Great Wakering
Churchend
130

A127
BASILDON
142/143
A1015
144/145
SOUTH BENFLEET
A13
146/147
A1159
148/149
150/151
River Roach

SOUTHEND-ON-SEA

/161
A130
162/163
CANVEY ISLAND
164/165
166/167
168
Stanford-le-Hope A1014
Coryton

Allhallows-on-Sea
st Tilbury
Cliffe
A228
Grain
SHEERNESS
Minster

Kingsnorth
River Medway
Leysdown-on-Sea

A226
A2
ROCHESTER
1
2
GILLINGHAM
Lower Halstow
A249
WHITSTABL[...]
A228
M2
CHATHAM
A2
SITTINGBOURNE
Conver
A229
A278
A2[...]

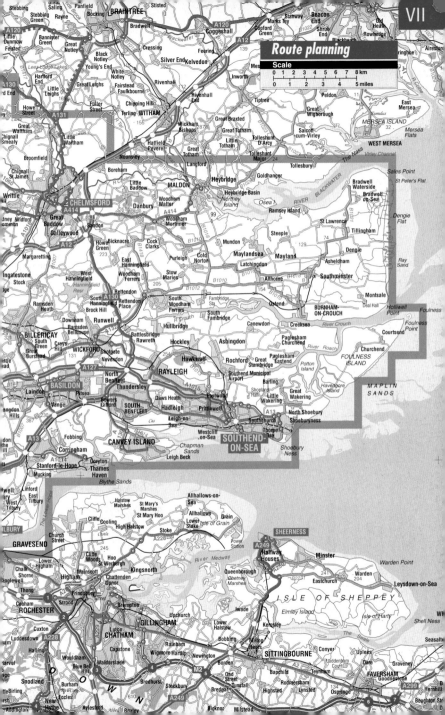

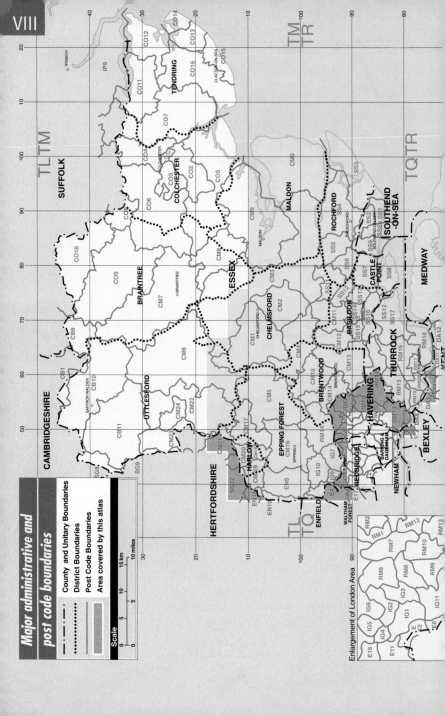

Major administrative and post code boundaries

Scale

County and Unitary Boundaries
District Boundaries
Post Code Boundaries
Area covered by this atlas

Enlargement of London Area

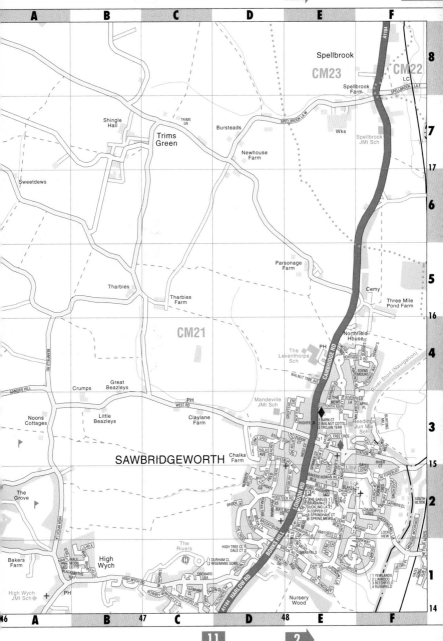

1

A B C D E F

8 Wallbury

STADDLES

BARKERS MEAD 1
GEORGE GREEN VILLAS 2
REDBRICK ROW 3

Beadle Common

Monksbury Farm

Little Hallingbury

Lock Farm

Sewage Works

POST OFFICE COTTS

Little Hallingbury CE Prim Sch

Nursery

GOOSE LA

7 Millhide Common

Gaston House

Gaston Common

Sutton Acres

Wright's Green

WRIGHTS GREEN LA

17 River Stort (Navigation)

Gaston Green

Mott's Green

6 Tednambury Farm

Mill (dis)

Little Bursteads

CM22

Little Hallingbury Park

Little Hallingbury Hall

5 South House Farm

Harcamlow Way

PH

Broadcroft

16 Spill Timbers Wood

Stone Hall

STORTFORD RD

4 Kecksy's Bridge

Camp Farm

Round Spring

Eighteenacre Spring

3 Great Hyde Hall

Oak Spring

Little Hyde Hall

Wren's Spring

FORGE COTTS

Sawbridgeworth

SAWBRIDGEWORTH RD

15 LC

1 PRIORS CT
2 WATERSIDE PL

Cowick

CM21

2 THE MEADOWS

Quickbury Farm

Stort Valley Way

B183

THE FOUR ACRES

MEADOW

SHEERING MILL LA

PO

Lower Sheering

Gladwyns

1 LADY PRIOR

MOORLANDS REACH

THE STREET

Shrubbs

Sheering CE Prim Sch

B183

PO

14

49 A B 50 C D 51 E F

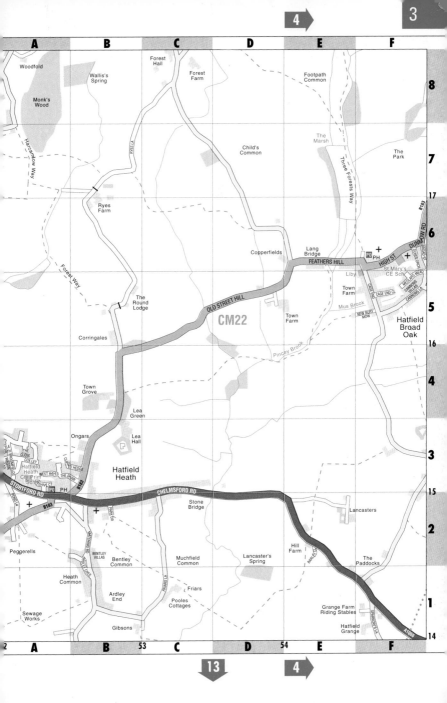

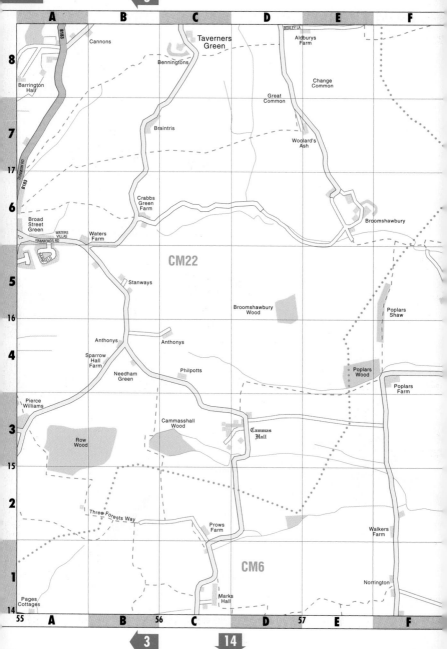

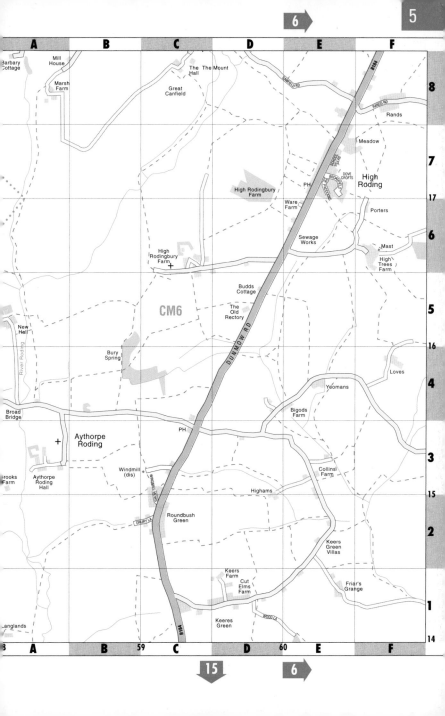

	A	B	C	D	E	F

8

Barnston House

Proverbs Green

Birds

Bishop's Green

PH

Little Garnetts

Great Garnetts

Broadgates

CM6

Mudwall

7

Attridge's Farm

Andrews

County Farm

Shooters Hatch

17

Shooters Hatch Farm

Barnfield

Crow Wood

Poplar Cottage

Poplar Farm

Sworders

6

Peakins

Ellis Farm

Wr Twr

Tree Field

Dobb's Wood

Chimballs

Bushbarns

Maidens

Green Street

CM3

5

Pentlowend

16

Callis Wood

Greens Farm

CM1

Sawkins

4

Folks & Crows

Hopkins

BELLHOUSE VILLAS

Lewis Cottage

3

Peartree Cottage

Parsonage Farm

Lewis's

Hill Farm

Sewage Works

Parsonage Brook

15

Slough Bridge

Parsonage Farm

OLD VICARAGE CL.

STAGDEN CROSS VILLAS

ST MARY'S BGLWS

KEEPERS CL.

THE STREET

Stagden Cross

2

Trotters Farm

PH

High Easter

Hayden's

1

Lower House

Essex Way

The Elms

14

| 61 | A | B | 62 | C | | D | 63 | E | | F |

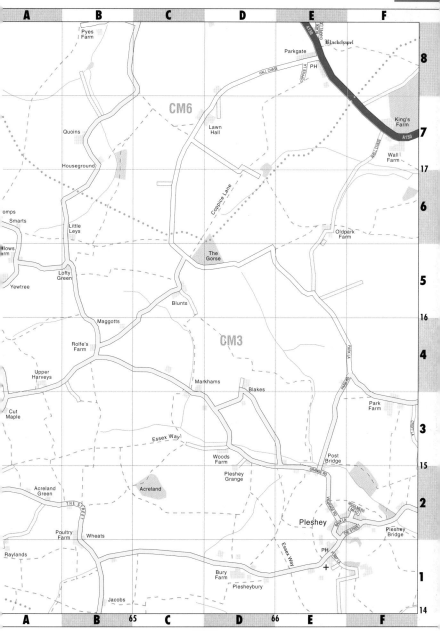

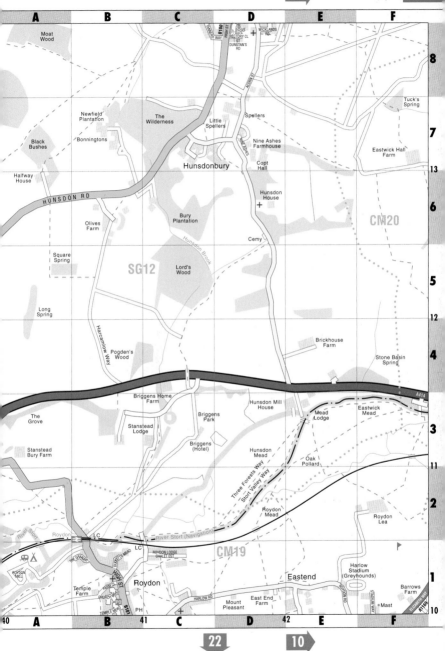

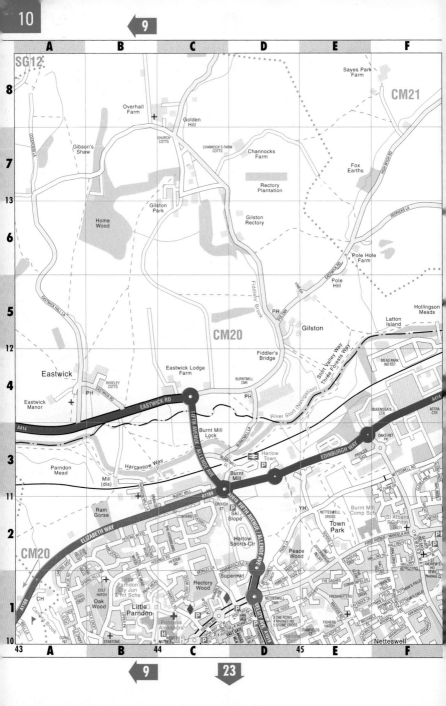

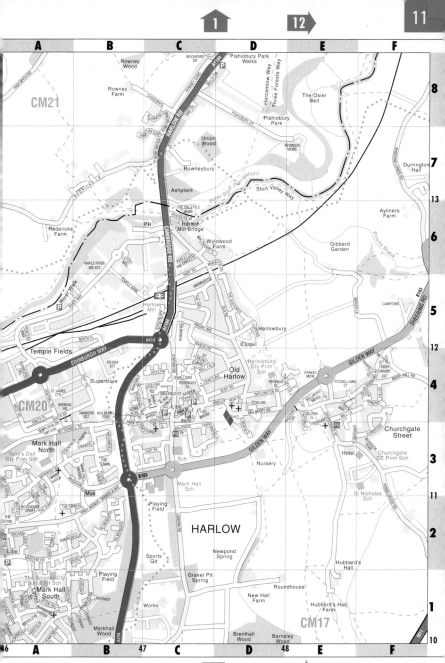

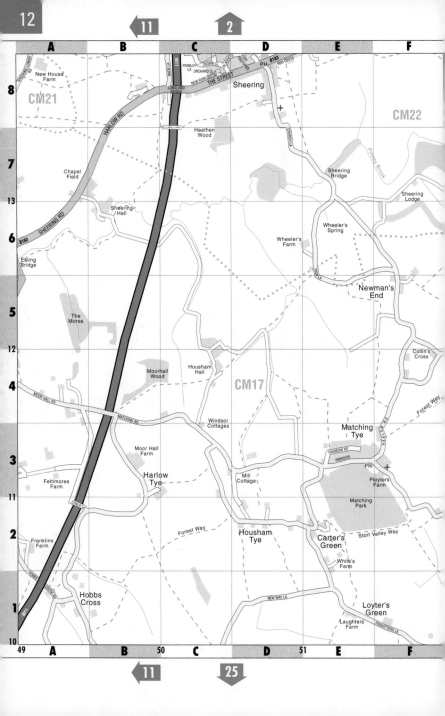

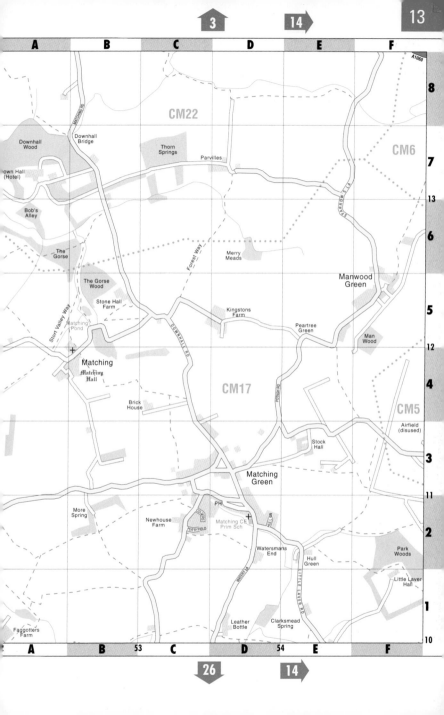

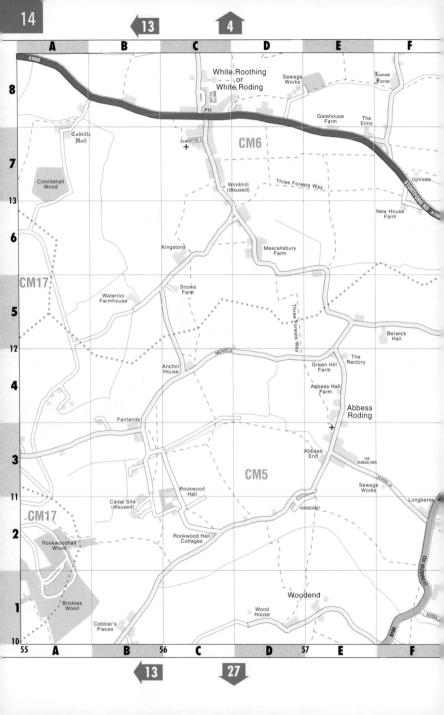

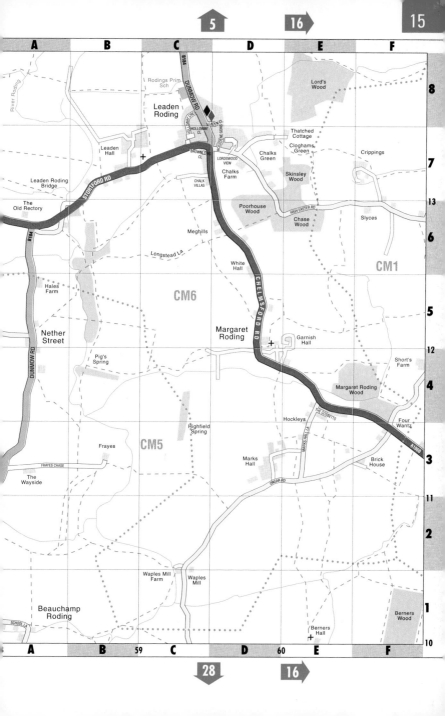

A B C D E F

8

7

13

6

5

12

4

3

11

2

1

10

River Roding

Rodings Prim Sch

B184

DUNMOW RD

Leaden Roding

HOLLOWAY CL

LEADEN CL

Leaden Hall

BROWNLOW CL

HORSEENE GDNS

LORDSWOOD VIEW

Leaden Roding Bridge

STORTFORD RD

CHALK VILLAS

Chalks Farm

Chalks Green

Thatched Cottage

Cloghams Green

Crippings

Skinsley Wood

Leaden Roding Bridge

The Old Rectory

B184

DUNMOW RD

Meghills

Longstead La

White Hall

Poorhouse Wood

Chase Wood

HIGH EASTER RD

Slyces

CM1

CM6

Hales Farm

Nether Street

Pig's Spring

CHELMSFORD RD

Margaret Roding

Garnish Hall

Short's Farm

Margaret Roding Wood

Four Wantz

A1060

Highfield Spring

CM5

Frayes

FRAYES CHASE

The Wayside

Hockleys

THE SCISBETTS

MARKS HALL LA

Marks Hall

Brick House

ONGAR RD

Waples Mill Farm

Waples Mill

Beauchamp Roding

SCHOOL LA

Berners Hall

Berners Wood

59 60

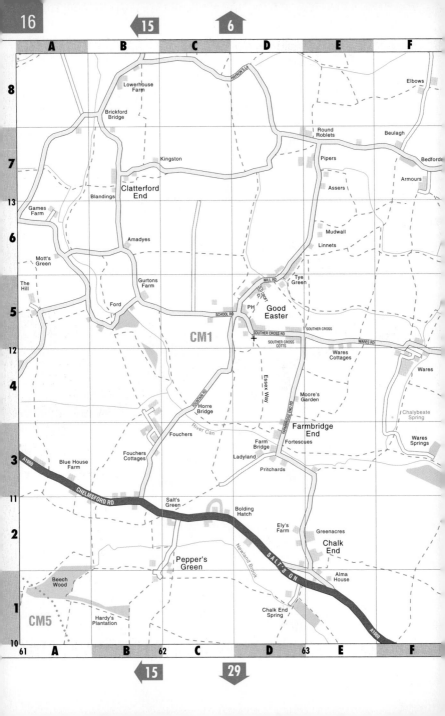

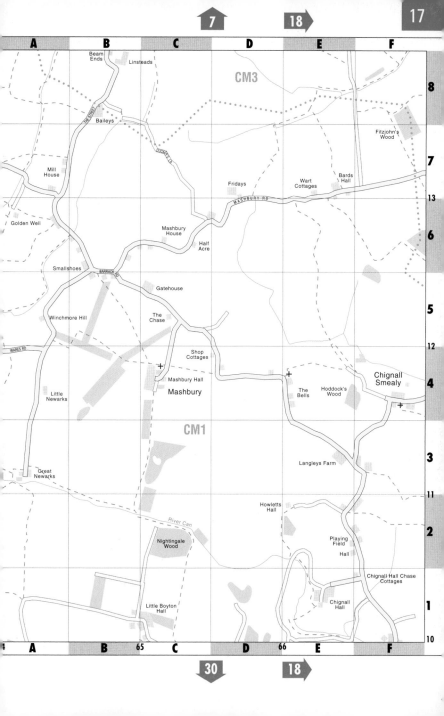

CM3

Beam Ends
Linsteads

Baileys

Mill House

Golden Well

Smallshoes

Winchmore Hill

WARES RD

Little Newarks

Great Newarks

THE STREET

DOCKETTS LA

Fridays

Mashbury House

Half Acre

Gatehouse

The Chase

Shop Cottages

Mashbury Hall

Mashbury

CM1

Nightingale Wood

River Can

Little Boyton Hall

MASHBURY RD

Wart Cottages

Bards Hall

Fitzjohn's Wood

BARRACK RD

The Bells

Hoddock's Wood

Chignall Smealy

Langleys Farm

Howletts Hall

Playing Field

Hall

Chignall Hall Chase Cottages

Chignall Hall

8
7
13
6
5
12
4
3
11
2
1
10

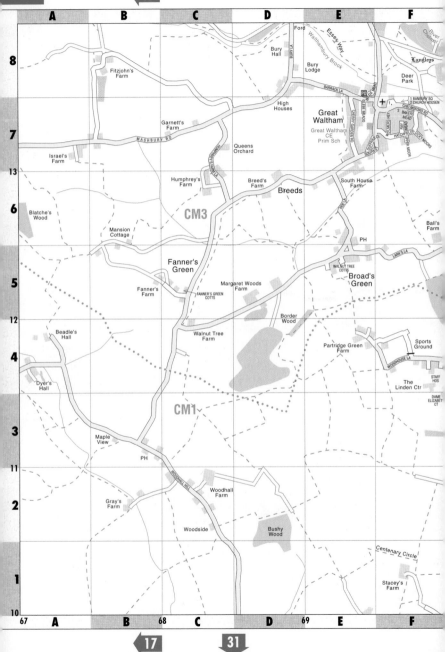

17

A **B** **C** **D** **E** **F**

8

Ford

Walthambury Brook

Essex Way

River Chelmer

Langleys

Bury Hall

Bury Lodge

Deer Park

BARRACK LA

High Houses

Great Waltham

1 BANBURY SQ
2 CHURCH HOUSES

Great Waltham CE Prim Sch

Garnett's Farm

7

MASHBURY RD

Queens Orchard

13

Israel's Farm

Humphrey's Farm

Breed's Farm

Breeds

South House Farm

Blatche's Wood

6

CM3

Ball's Farm

Mansion Cottage

PH

Fanner's Green

Broad's Green

LARKS LA

WALNUT TREE COTTS

5

Fanner's Farm

FANNER'S GREEN COTTS

Margaret Woods Farm

12

Border Wood

Beadle's Hall

4

Walnut Tree Farm

Partridge Green Farm

Sports Ground

WOODHOUSE LA

Dyer's Hall

The Linden Ctr

STAFF HOS

DAME ELIZABETH CT

CM1

3

Maple View

PH

11

Woodhall Farm

2

Gray's Farm

Woodside

Bushy Wood

Centenary Circle

1

Stacey's Farm

10

67 **A** **B** 68 **C** **D** 69 **E** **F**

17 31

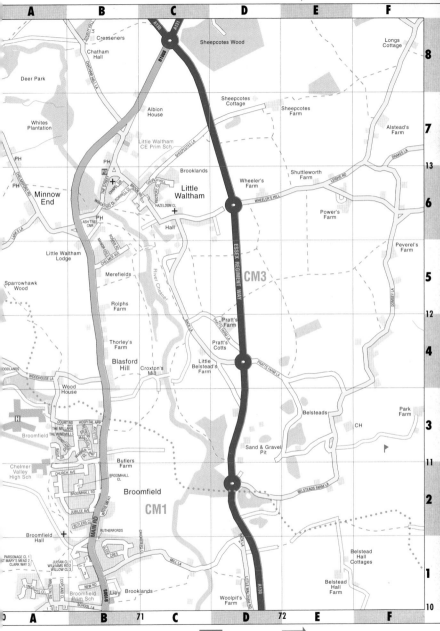

19

A | B | C | D | E | F

8

Chopping's Wood

Noake's House

Noake's Farm

Lawns Farm

Ringer's Wood

7

Little Drakes

Bird's Farm

DRAKES LA

Drake's Farm

Works

Russel Green House

13

Russell Green

6

Brent Hall

Stocks Farm

5

GM3

Stocks Cottages

Porter's Wood

Little Holts

12

Works

P

Holts Farm

Boreham Airfield (disused)

4

WALTHAM RD

WALLACE'S LA

Sand & Gravel Pit

Wallace's Farm Cottages

3

Park Farm

Walford House

Mount Maskall

11

2

Centenary Circle

GENERALS LA

The Grove

Brick House Farm

BOREH IND ES

1

New Hall (Convent)

P

BULLS LODGE COTTS

Bulls Lodge

GWYN CL 1
ROSEMARY COTTS 2
ARMONDE CL 3
MEADOWSIDE CT 4
SEABROOK GDNS 5

MAIN RD

A12

B1137

ALLENS CL

CLAYPITS RD

10

19 33

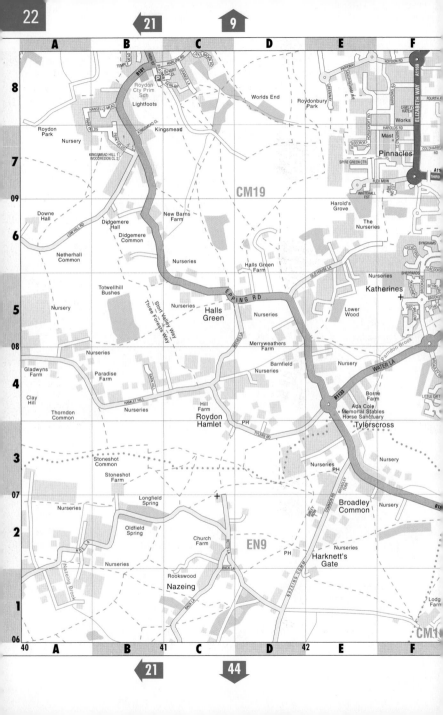

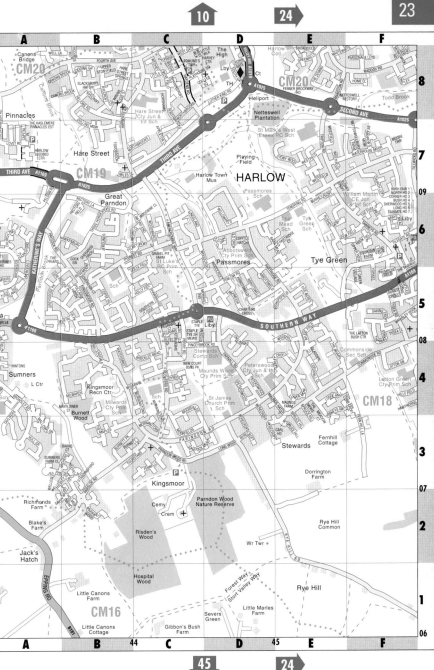

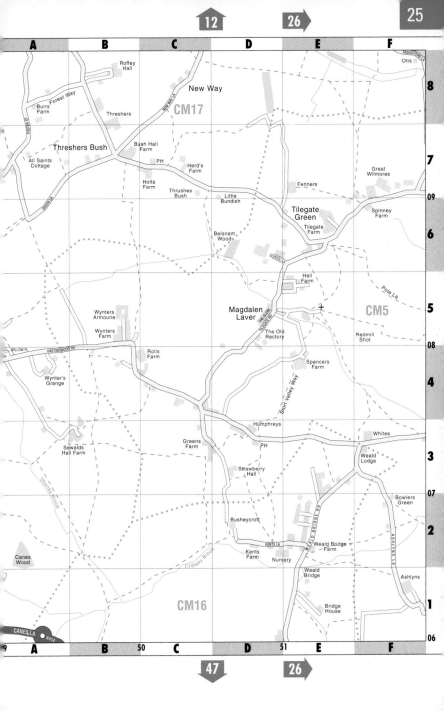

A **B** **C** **D** **E** **F**

FAGGOTERS LA

Otis

Roffey
Hall

8

New Way

Burrs
Farm

NEW HALL LA

CM17

Threshers

Bush Hall
Farm

7

All Saints
Cottage

Threshers Bush

PH

Herd's
Farm

Great
Wilmores

Holts
Farm

Thrushes
Bush

Little
Bundish

Fenners

09

Belsnam
Wood

Tilegate
Green

Spinney
Farm

6

Tilegate
Farm

SCHOOL LA

Pole La

Hall
Farm

CM5

5

Wynters
Armourie

Magdalen
Laver

THE LAVER

TILEGATE RD

Redmill
Shot

08

Wynters
Farm

The Old
Rectory

WILLOW PL

HASTINGWOOD RD

Rolls
Farm

Spencers
Farm

4

Wynter's
Grange

Short Valley Way

Sewalds
Hall Farm

Humphreys

Whites

Greens
Farm

PH

Weald
Lodge

3

Strawberry
Hall

Bowlers
Green

07

Busheycroft

2

Canes
Wood

Shering Brook

KENTS LA

Weald Bridge
Farm

ASHLYNS LA

Kents
Farm

WEALD BRIDGE RD

Cripsey Brook

Nursery

Weald
Bridge

Ashlyns

CM16

Bridge
House

1

06

CANES LA
A414

9

A **50** **B** **C** **D** **51** **E** **F**

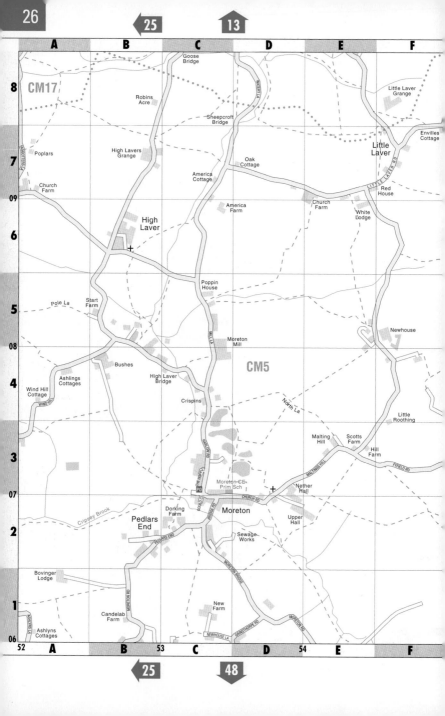

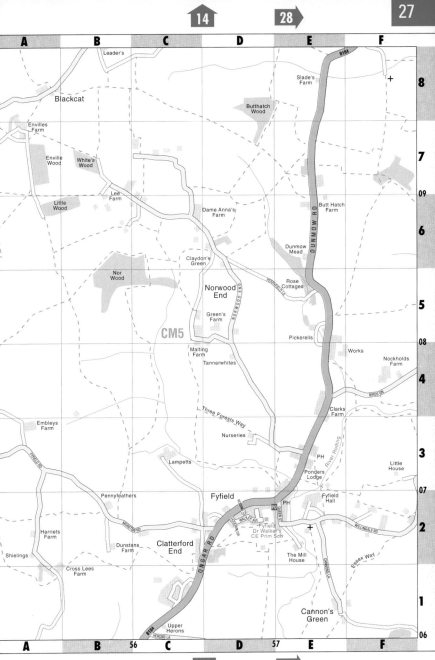

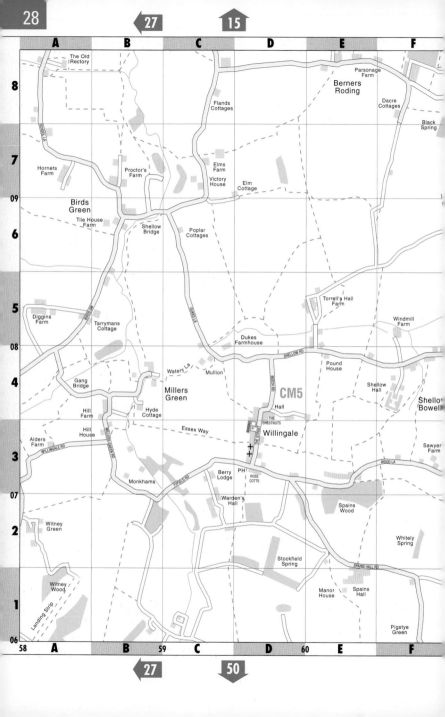

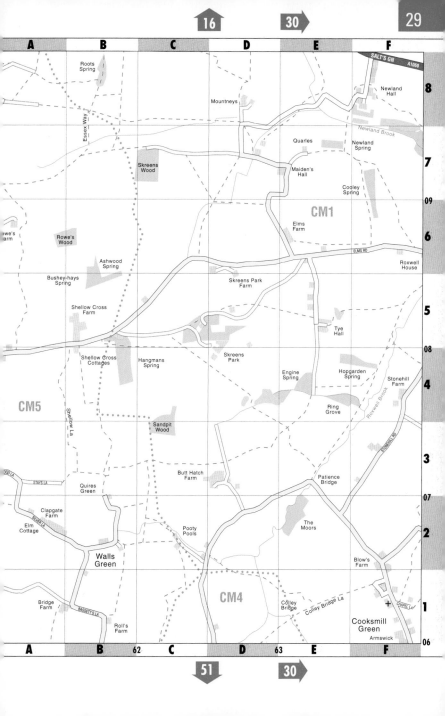

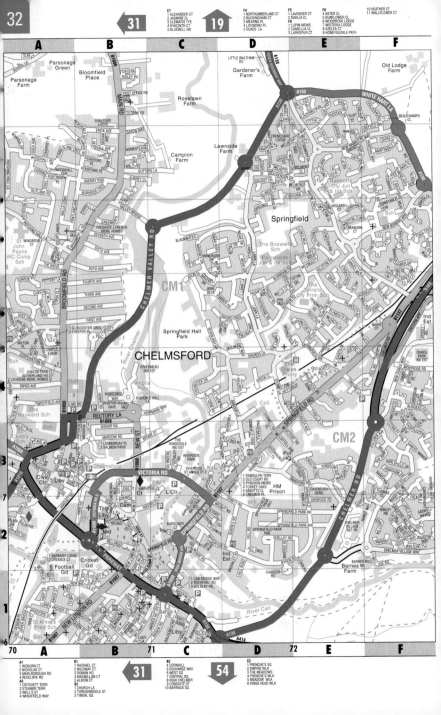

8
7
09
6
5
08
4
3
07
2
1
06

A B C D E F

Mulberries

Culverts Cottages

Brakey Wood

Culvert's Farm

Belstead Cottages

World's End Cottage

Rickstones

MOWDEN HALL LA

Gardener's Farm

Botter's Farm

Multum in Parvo

Chelmer & Blackwater Navigation

Weir

Paper Mill Lock

Paper Mill Bridge

Bassett's Farm

River Chelmer

New Wood

Brickwell Wood

CHELMER LA

Coleraines

TOFTS CHASE

WICKHAY COTTS

SPRING CL

JARVIS FIELD

Walters Cottage

Tofts

Holybreds Wood

PH

Bassett's Wood

+

Little Baddow Hall

Holybreds Farm

HOLYBREDS LA

Warren Farm

Scrub Wood

CM3

The Hoppet

Cuckoos

Little BADDOW

+

Gibbs

CHAPEL LA

COLAM LA

Burghfields Farm

PASTURE FIELD

The Warren

SPRING ELMS LA

Duke's Orchard

HURRELLS LA

Waterhall

Belle Vue Farm

PH

CHER FIELD

MILL LA

POSTMANS LA

OAKLANDS DRI

Birch Wood

Elm Green Sch

PARSONAGE LA

New Lodge

NEW LODGE CHASE

Blake's Wood

Old Riffhams

RIFFHAMS CHASE

COMMON LA

Pheasanthouse Wood

Long Spring Wood

Nature Reserve

Long Wood

FIR TREE LA

HANTONS LA

WOODSIDE

Great Graces

GRACES LA

The White House

Ling Wood

Poors' Piece

Hall Wood

Great Graces Farm

RIFFHAMS LA

Riffhams

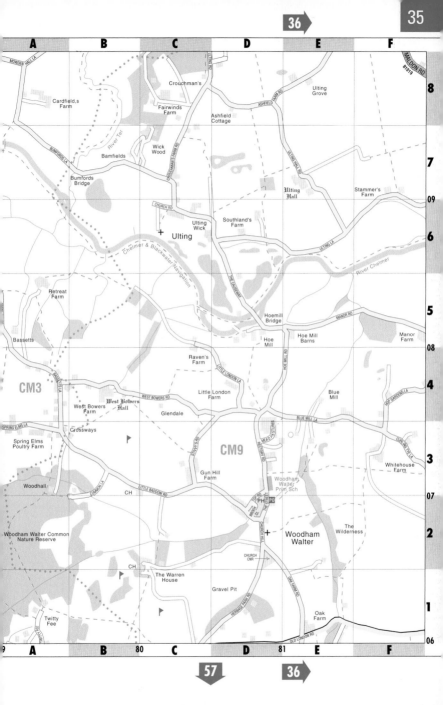

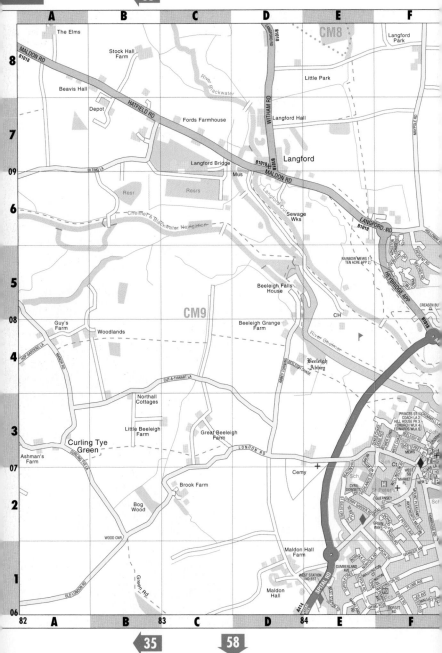

A   B   C   D   E   F

CHURCH LA

B1026

8

Little London
Farm

LITTLE TOTHAM RD

Folly Faunts
House

Falcons Hall
Farm

Goldhanger
House

7

BLIND LA

BRICK
COTTAGES

WASH LA

Chappel
Farm

MALDON RD

HALL DRIVE

PO

Agricultural/Domestic
Mus

PH

Goldhanger

09

HEAD ST

FISH ST

FEATHER DL

PH

6

Rook
Hall

Cobb's
Farm

THISTLEY CL

CM9

5

Wash
Bridge

Gardener's
Farm

Bound's
Farm

08

BARROW
MARSH

Vaulty
Manor

GOLDHANGER RD

4

B1026

Red
Hill

Cvn
Pks

DEER RD

Sewage
Works

3

Mill
Beach

Collier's Reach

Hilly Pool
Point

07

Decoy
Point

Causeway

2

River Blackwater

West Point

Osea
Island

Northey
Island

1

06

88   A   B   89   C   D   90   E   F

A   B   C   D   E   F

Lower
Grove

New
Barn

8

Wycke
Farm

Highams
Farm

Longwick
Farm

7

Bowstead Brook

09

Lauriston
Farm

Joyce's
Farm

6

CM9

Gore
Saltings

5

08

Goldhanger Creek

4

River Blackwater

3

07

The Stumble

CM0

2

Osea
Island

Works

East
Point

Osea
Farm

1

Wr
Twr

06

A   B 92 C   D 93 E   F

39

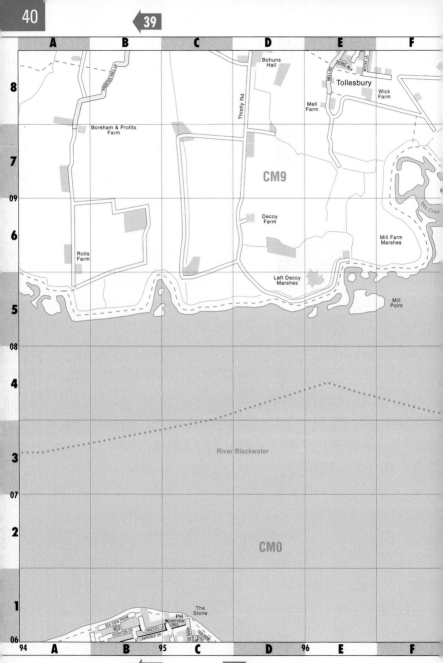

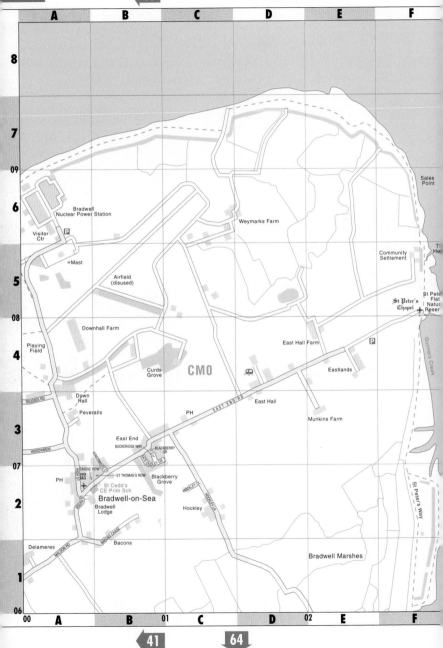

A   B   C   D   E   F

8

7

09

6

Bradwell
Nuclear Power Station

Visitor
Ctr

P

Weymarks Farm

Community
Settlement

T
He

Mast

5

Airfield
(disused)

St Pete
Flat
Natur
Reser

St Peter's
Chapel

08

Downhall Farm

Playing
Field

East Hall Farm

P

CMO

4

Curds
Grove

Eastlands

Gunners Creek

TRUSSES RD

Down
Hall

PH

EAST END RD

East Hall

Peveralls

3

WOODYARDS

East End

BUCKERIDGE WAY

Munkins Farm

PH

BLACKBERRY
GR

KINGSKNOLL CT

ST CEDD'S RD

CAIDGE ROW

ST THOMAS'S ROW

Blackberry
Grove

HOCKLEY CT

HOCKLEY

PH

St Cedd's
CE Prim Sch

Bradwell-on-Sea

2

SOUTH ST

Bradwell
Lodge

Hockley

St Peter's Way

Delameres

BIRDSNE CHASE

MALDON RD

Bacons

Bradwell Marshes

1

06

00   A   B   01   C   D   02   E   F

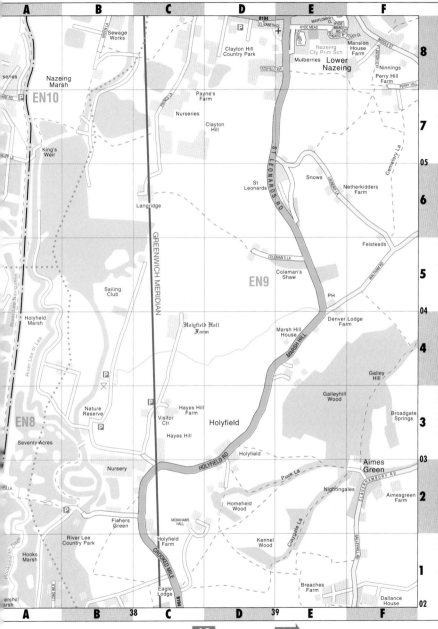

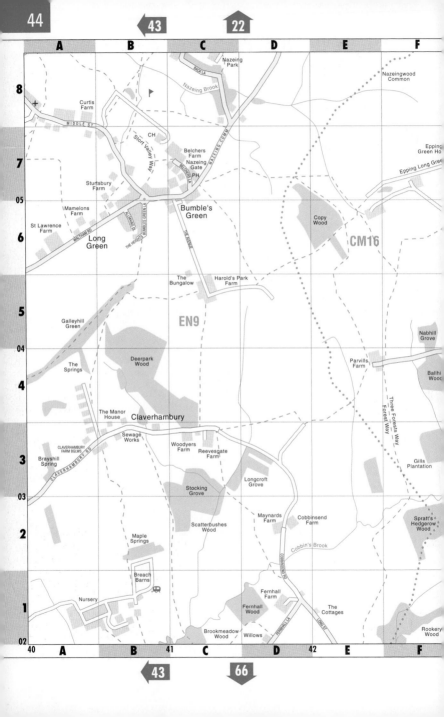

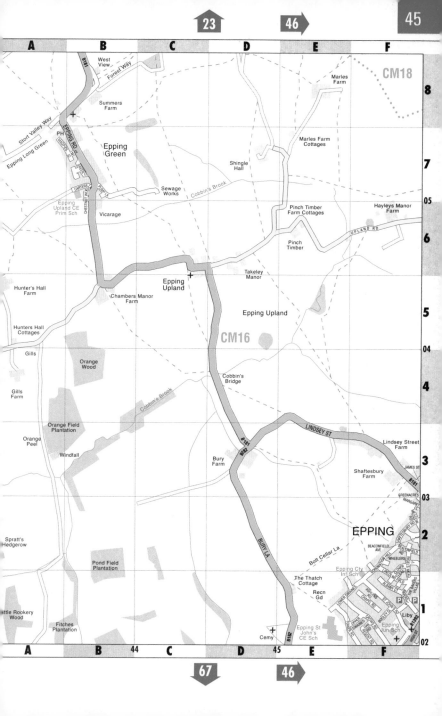

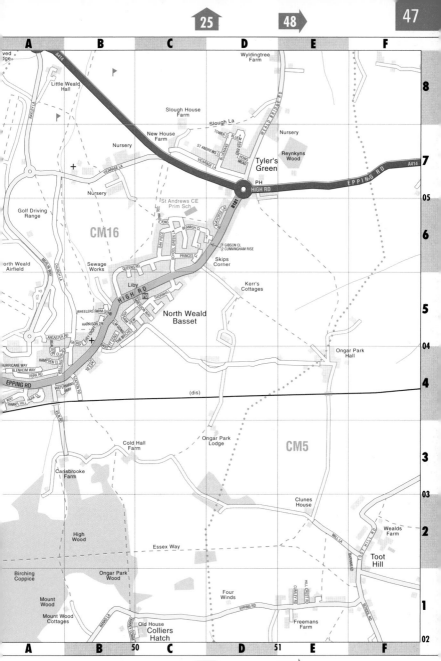

47
26

	A	B	C	D	E	F

8

Great Notts

Hobban's Farm

Wood Farm

Bundish Spring

Nursery

Bobbingworth

Bovinger Hall

Sayers Farm

7
A414 Bovinger

Lower Bobbingworth Green

Round Spring

05

Blake Hall Gardens

Long Walk

Lodge

Blake Hall

6

Waterloo Bridge

EPPING RD

Bridge House

Shelley Bridge

Dewley Wood

Bilsdens Cottages

Shelley

5

Pickle's Gardens

Bilsdens

Water End Farm

BLAKE HALL RD

Perrills

Shelley Cty Prim Sch

04

Miller's Grove

(dis)

CM5

The Rosary

Ackingford Bridge

A4

AUKINGFORD

4

CHIPPING ONGAR

New Barn Cottages

BONES

3

Greensted House

Little Thorbens

PENSON'S LA

Greensted Green

Ongar Wood

Greensted Hall

Hardings Farm

03

Greensted Wood

Essex Way

Hall Farm

Greensted Log Church

Greensted

East Lodge

FOXT HILL RD

2

DRAPER'S CNR

GREENSTED RD

Lodge Farm

THE SPINNEY

1

Widow's Farm

PH

Chipping Ongar Cty Prim Sch

Clatterford End

MUTTON ROW

PARKLAND WAY

Burrows Farm

FOXT HILL RD

Newhouse

Three Forests Way

02

52	A	B	53	C	D	54	E	F

47
70

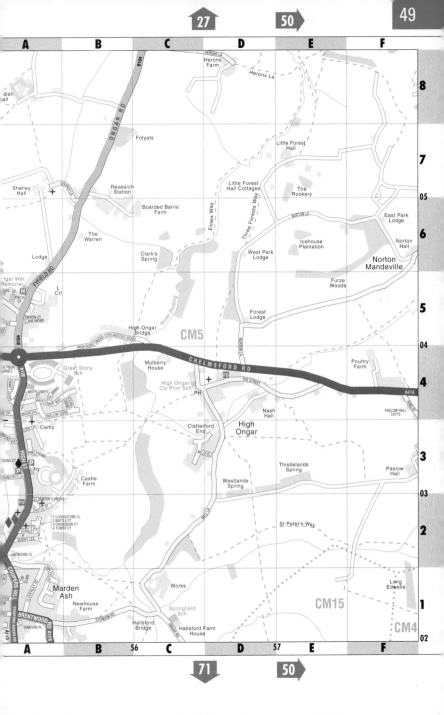

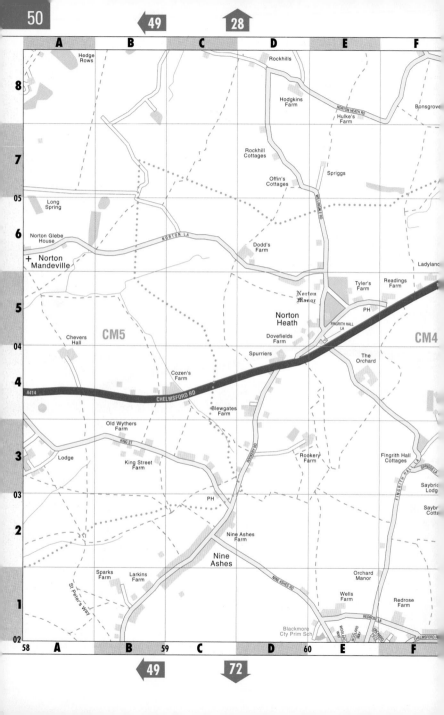

A   B   C   D   E   F

8

CM5

Brookend
Farm

Butlers
Farm

Radley Green
Farm

Colleybridge
Farm

Radley
Green

Home
Farm

Red
House

PIGSTYE GREEN RD

ords

Lucas's La

Parnells

Bassett's
Farm

BASSETT'S LA

RADLEY GREEN RD

RADLEY GREEN RD

PH

Hand's
Farm

Ewson's
Farm

Brainwood
Farm

7

05

ONGAR RD

A414

Hawkin Smith's
Farmhouse

PH

WEST RD

Horsfrith Park
Farm

Ewson's
Bridge

6

CM1

Horsfrithpark
Wood

Ewson's Brook

Fithlers Hall
Farm

5

CM4

Ward's
Farm

04

HIGHWOOD RD

4

Cat & Kittens
Cottages

Gorrell's
Farm

Awes
Farm

POOL LA

Fingrith Hall
Farm

Old
Barns

OLD BARNS LA

Highwood
Cottages

3

Budd's
Farm

03

COCK LA

Ellis
Wood

METSONS LA

NIGHTINGALE RD

BARROW FARM RD

Barrow
Farm

High
Woods

2

Parsons
Spring

Barrow
Wood

Highwood
Cottage

BRIDGES LA

Sprigg's
Farm

Quince
Hall

Birch
Spring

Monk's & Barrow's
Farm

1

CHELMSFORD RD

Howlett's
Hall

Deerslade
Wood

02

A   B   62   C   D   63   E   F

Wellington House
Cooksmill Nursery
Landview House
Four Gables
Wyse's Cottage
Montague Farm
Loves Green
Highwood Cty Prim Sch
Chalk Hill
High Woods
Whitegates
Redindyke Farm
Wells & Sheds

Little Moor Hall
Lady Grove
Bramwood Farm
Southridge Farm
Nursery
PH
WOODSIDE COTTS
Writtle Park Farm
Writtle Park
Parkponds Wood
Hockley Shaw

CM4

ONGAR RD W
Range Cottage
ONGAR RD
Little Oxney Green
GREENBURY WAY (WRITTLE BY-PASS)
A414
CAUSEWAY COTTS
Halfway House
Lee Cottages
Roper's Farm
Montpelier's Farm
Lee Farm
Lee Wood
Edney Common
Sewage Works
CM1
Jordan's Farm
NATHAN'S LA
Little Edney Wood
Great Edney Wood
Mast
Baker's Wood
Writtlepark Wood
Furness Wood
Coptfold Hall
King Wood
Coptfoldhall Farm
Park Lodge
Coptfold Farm Cottages
Furness Farm
Chatterbox Wood
Bearman's Farm
Dawes Farm
Handley Green Farm
Furze Hill
Hotel
IVY BARNS LA

A414
WYSE'S RD
SPARROW'S LA
BLUEBELL'S MEAD
COCK LA
BRIDGEFORD RD
WRITTLE RD

THE GREENWAY
HIGHWOOD RD
HIGHWOOD RD

THE SHRUBBERIES
ROLLESTONS

A   B   C   D   E   F

8   7   05   6   5   04   4   3   03   2   02   1

A B C D E F

CM3

8

Water
Works

Manor
Farm

MILL
COTTS

Old Hare Wood

The
White House

MALDON RD

Sandon
Bridge

GRACE'S
CROSS

A414

A414 MAIN RD A414

7

A414

Grace's
Cross

Sandon Brook

05

Sandon
Lodge

The
Sandon Sch

Bridge
Farm

Sandon

WOODHILL RD

6

Lower
Green

CABD'S RD LA

Mayes
Farm

Dealtrees
Farm

CM2

SOUTHEND RD A114

LADYMILL LA

Gravel Pit

5

Hotel

Pontlands
Farm

Spare
Bridge

04

CM3

The
Grove

Sandon
Hall

BLIND LA

SPOREHAMS LA

Hillview

4

Gingerbreadhall
Bridge

ST SWITHINS
COTTS

Howe
Farm

White Lodge
Farm

Butt's Green

3

Great
Mascalls

Sandon Brook

Howe Green

SOUTHEND RD

EAST HANNINGFIELD RD

03

BROOK LA

Little
Sir Hughes

Three
Oaks

Southlands
Farm

Grove
Farm

2

Little
Mascalls

Great
Sir Hughes

Rowlands

A130 SOUTHEND RD

1

CM3

02

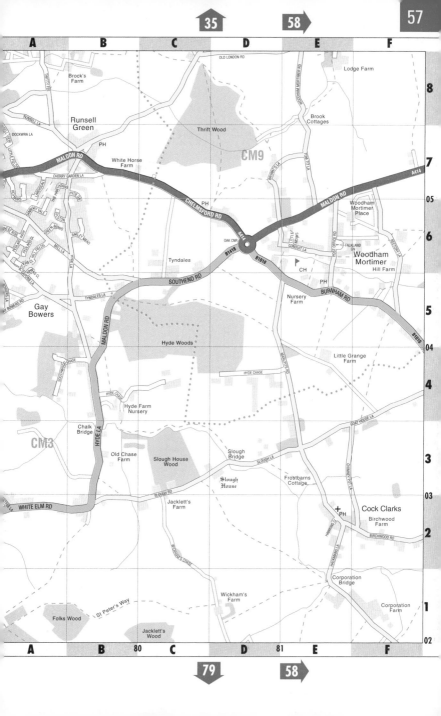

A · **B** · **C** · **D** · **E** · **F**

8

OLD LONDON RD

Brock's Farm

Lodge Farm

Runsell Green

Thrift Wood

Brook Cottages

CM9

7

MALDON RD

PH

White Horse Farm

CHELMSFORD RD

A414

MALDON RD

DR TTL RD

05

PH

Woodham Mortimer Place

OAK CNR

A414

B1418

B1010

Little St Mary's

St Mary's

Post Office

FALKLAND GN

Woodham Mortimer

6

CONDUIT LA

CH

Hill Farm

Tyndales

SOUTHEND RD

PH

BURNHAM RD

B1010

Gay Bowers

MALDON RD

TYNDALES LA

Nursery Farm

5

SOUTHDOWN CHASE

Hyde Woods

Little Grange Farm

04

HYDE CHASE

4

HYDE CHASE

MALDON RD

Hyde Farm Nursery

GOAT HOUSE LA

Chalk Bridge

HYDE LA

CM3

Old Chase Farm

Slough House Wood

Slough Bridge

SLOUGH LA

CHURCH POTT LA

3

WHITE ELM RD

SLOUGH RD

Slough House

Frostbarns Cottage

03

HAMMONDS LA

PH

Cock Clarks

Jacklett's Farm

Birchwood Farm

HACKMANS LA

BIRCHWOOD RD

2

WOODHAM CHASE

Corporation Bridge

St Peter's Way

Folks Wood

Wickham's Farm

Corporation Farm

1

Jacklett's Wood

02

A · **B** · 80 · **C** · **D** · 81 · **E** · **F**

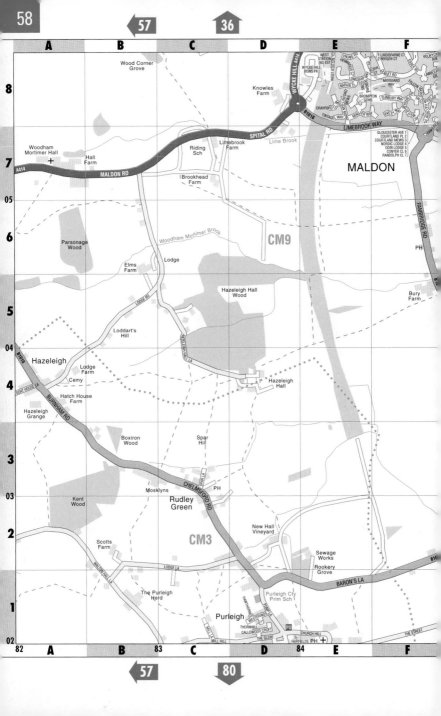

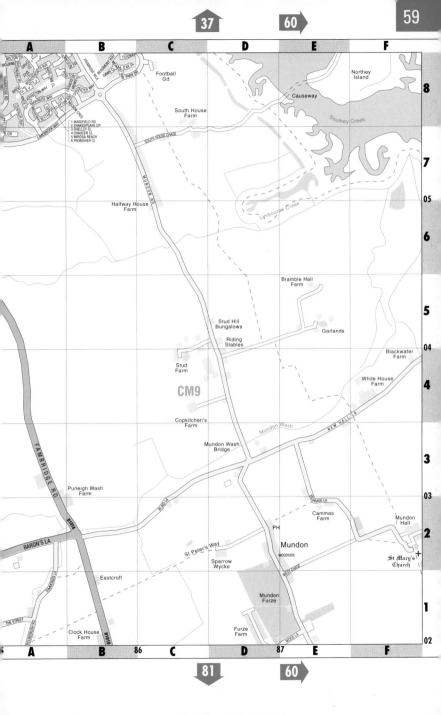

Northey
Island

8

Southey Creek

7

05

Cooper's
Creek

6

CM0

Iltney
Farm

5

New Hall
Farm

Freshfields

The
Bungalow

CM9

04

Oaklea

Lawling Creek

Brookmead
Farm

4

Brick House
Farm

3

03

2

RUSSELLS CHASE

SEA VIEW RD

Mundon Creek

Marina

The
Plantation

THE ESPLANADE

NORTH DR

PORTLACE

IMPERIAL AVE

PH

DERBY CL

DEF

1

02

St Peter's Way

CM3

GEORGE
CHURCHILL

WEST AVE

PH

THE DRIVE

Maylandsea

BARTLETT CL

88   A   B   89   C   D   90   E   F

A B C D E F

CM9

The Chase

Pier

Stansgate Abbey
Farm

8

Ramsey
Marsh

7

05

Mundon Stone
Point

Rainbow
Cottages

6

Steeplewick Farm
Cottage

Lawling Creek

Steeple Creek

STANSGATE RD

5

Canney
House

CM0

04

Mayland Creek

4

Gate House
Farm

3

St Peter's Way

Steeple
Hall

CANNEY RD

Steeple

PH
GARDENS RD

BRADWELL
RD

BETTS RD

PO
PH

03

Hill's
Farm

THE STREET

COUNCIL
OFFICES

Grange
Farm

MALDON RD

2

BALMORAL RD

CM3

NIPSELLS CHASE

Nipsells
Farm

Sewage
Wks

DUKE OF WORCESTER

HULL LANE WAY

MILL RD

BRAMLEY RD

HILL CREST

Bramble
Farm

DOCK RD

1

02

A B 92 C D 93 E F

St Lawrence

Ramsey Island

Ramsey Marsh

Steeplewick
Farm

St Lawrence Bay

BAY VIEW
WICK FARM
SEAWAY
HIGH VIEW
MOUNTVIEW DRIVE
SUNNY WAY
PO
BEACHY DR
MOUNTVIEW AVE
PH

Beacon Hill
Leisure Park

Beacon Hill
Farm

Sewage
Works

Mott's
Farm

BRADWELL RD

St Lawrence

St Lawrence
Hall
Wr Twr

CMO

St LAWRENCE HILL

Kings
Farm

STEEPLE RD

Black Horse
Farm

Brick House
Farm

SOUTHMINSTER RD

BRADWELL RD
STANDARD ST
IVY
COTTS

Poplars
Farm

The
Lodge

West
Newlands

East
Newlands

Batt's
Farm

BATT'S RD

Asheldham Brook

Moynes
Farm

Asheldham
Grange

A B C D E F

8
7
05
6
5
04
4
03
3
2
02
1

94 A 95 B C 96 D E F

8 Queen's Head (Motel)
Gracedale Farm
COUNCIL HOS
Mill End
COASTGUARD COTTS
Curry

MALDON RD

Highfield
7
Bradwell Hall
Bradwell Wick
MALDON RD

Bradwell Brook

Byhams
05

Bradwell Wick Nursery
Nut Grove
MARK RD
6
Middle Grove
Sampsons

Blackbirds
Tillingham Brook
BRADWELL RD
Mark Farm

CMO
5
East Hyde

St Peter's Way
ST LAWRENCE RD
BROOK RD
04

West Hyde
Tillingham Hall
NORTH ST
MARSH RD

Tillingham St Nicholas CE Prim Sch
WESSLEY CL
4
Stows Farm
Tillingham
BIRCH GDNS

VICARAGE LA
BIRCH RD
STOWE'S LA
CHAPEL LA
Vicarage
MARLBOROUGH AVE

REDDINGS LA
BAKERY CL
SOUTH ST

ENGLEFIELDS
3
Reddings Farm
Reddings
ORANGE RD
03

Hill Farm
PH
White Horse Farm

TILLINGHAM RD
gh House Farm
SOUTHMINSTER RD
2

rashes
Bacons
MAIN RD
GLBE LA

Mullingers
Glebe Farm
1

B1021
Dengie
02

A   B   C   D   E   F

8

Bradwell Marshes

Glebe
Farm

COOKLEY LA

7

Packards
Grove

Bradwell Brook

Sandbeach

05

Packards

MARK RD

Weatherwick

6

5

Shingleford

Dots &
Melons

MARSH RD

CMO

Marshhouse
Decoy Pond

04

4

Leggatts

MARSH RD

Marsh
House

3

Bridgemans
Farm

Tillingham Marshes

03

Jerry's
Farm

2

Midlands

Howe
Farm

Howe
Outfall

1

Crosby

GRANGE RD

Grange
Farm

BROADFIELDS RD

02

Small Gains

00   A   B   01   C   D   02   E   F

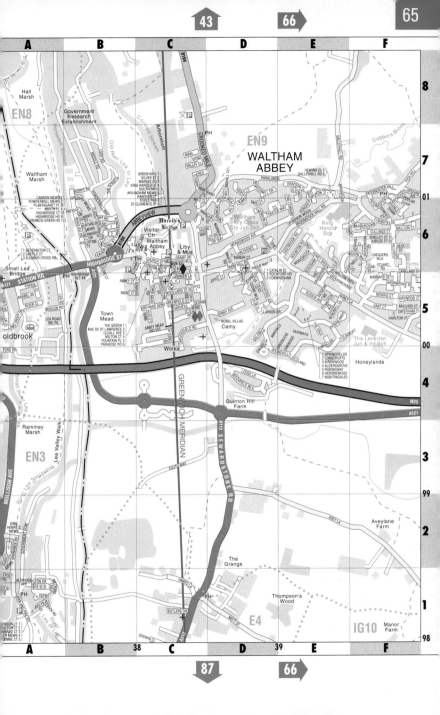

8

7

01

6

5

00

4

3

99

2

1

98

A
B
44
C
D
45
E
F

The White House
Home Farm
Copped Hall
Wood House
Griffin's Wood
New Farm
Creeds Farm
Creeds Cotts
Hotel
Ivy Chimneys
Ivy Chimneys Cty Prim Sch
Griffin's Wood
Griffin's Wood Cotts
Bell Common
Ladderstile Farm
Holly Cotts
HIGH RD
BURY LA
HIGH ST
Ivy Chimneys Rd
Bridge Hill
Park Cottages
The Warren
Warren Wood
Warren Lodge
Epping Thicks
CROWN HILL
Loreto Convent
Great Gregories Farm
Great Gregories La
Theydon Rd
Forest Dri
CH
Little Gregories
CM16
M25
Ambresbury Banks Fort
Centenary Wlk
EPPING RD
Little Gregories La
Piercing Hill
Long Running
Genesis Slade
Wansfell Coll
Piercing Hill
Theydon Bois Cty Prim Sch
Green Ride Lane
Jack's Hill
P
P
Oak Hill Farm
Birch Hall Farm
Birch Hall
PH
Theydon Bois
Liby
Coppice Row
Station App
PH
Theydon Bois
Parsonage Farm
Copley Plain
The Ditches Ride
Birch Wood
Ripley Grange
Redoak Wood
Gaunts Wood
The Heights 1
Willingale Ct 2
3 Elm Ct
4 Green View
Chester Cotts
Robert Daniels Ct
Abridge Rd
B172
Thrifts Hall Farm
Furze Ground
IG10
Gregson's Ride
Debden Green
Davenant Foundation Sch
Debden La
1 Garden Way
2 The Beacons
Theydon Park Rd

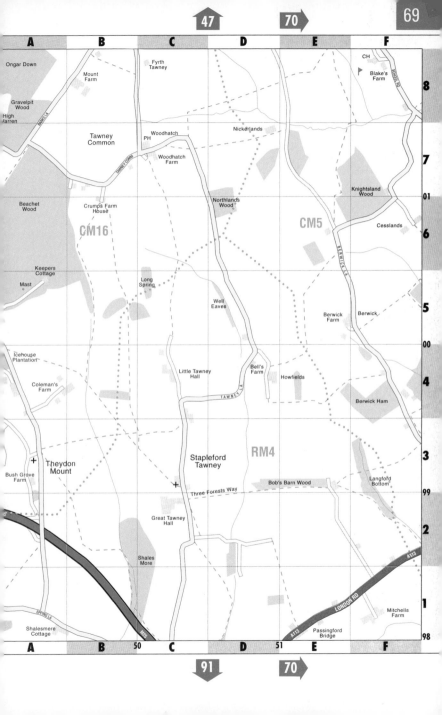

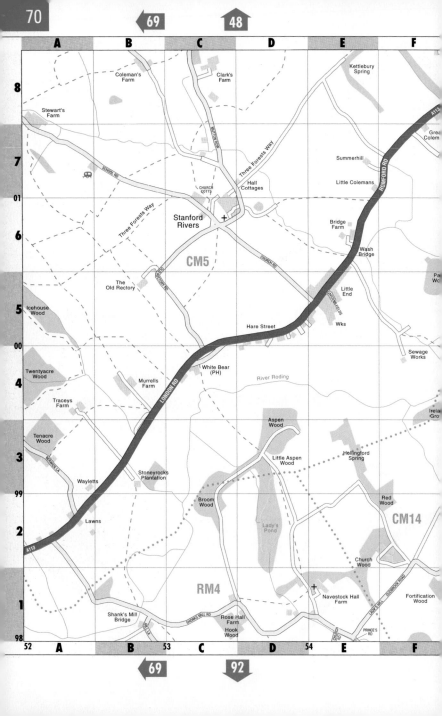

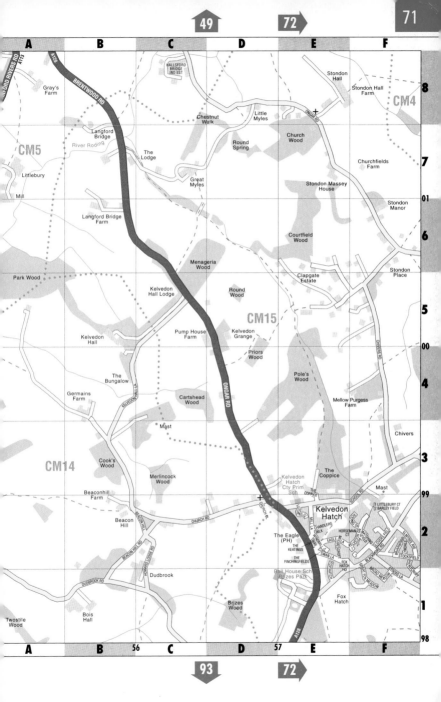

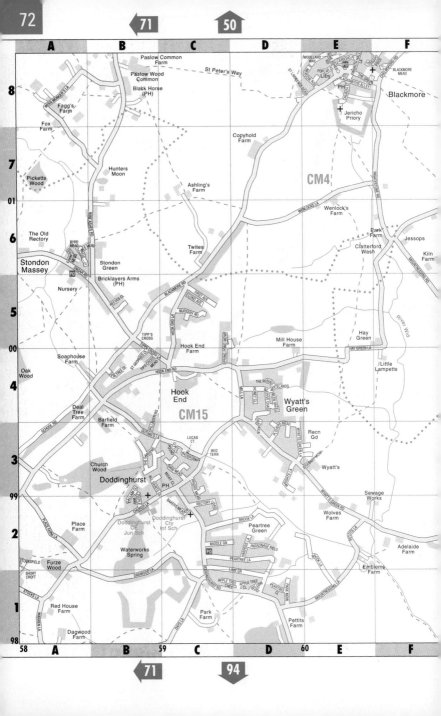

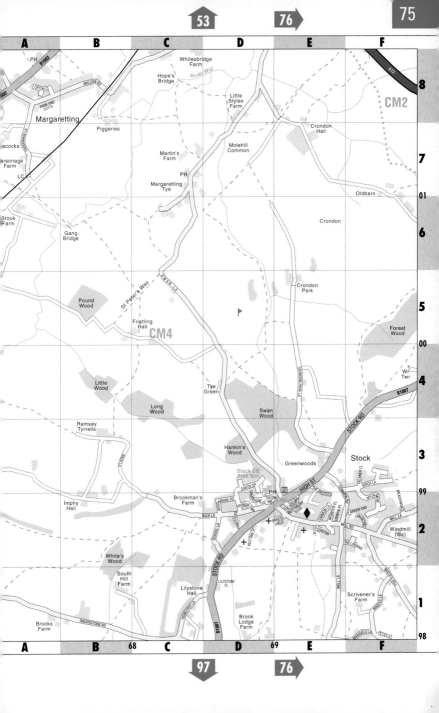

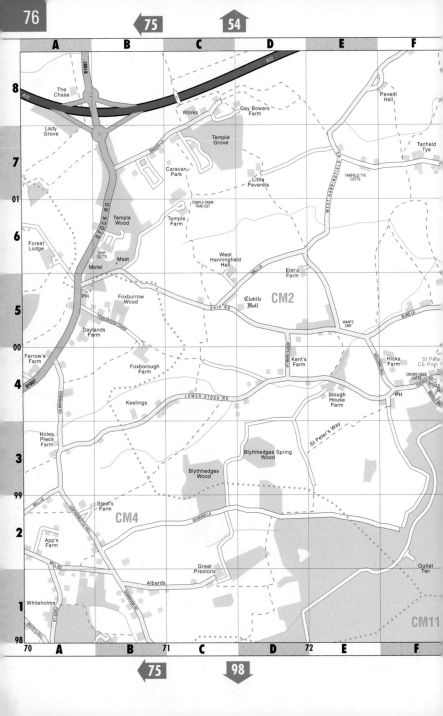

A B C D E F

8
Bluebell Wood

Little Claydons Farm

Downhouse

7
01

Bushy Wood

SOUTHEND RD

A130

OLD SOUTHEND RD

Ford
CM2
Patten's Farm

Hill Farm

6

Tinsley Farm

Tudor Farm

St Peter's Wlk

Hill Farm Cottages

Charvilles

PAN LA

5
00

Harvesters Farm

BLIND LA

Link House Farm

Doylands Farm

Barnard's Farm

PH

4

CHURCH LA

West Hanningfield

CHURCH RD

The Rectory

Canon Barns

MIDDLEMEAD

Bloodlands

CM3

BONNETTS AVE

A130

3
99

Works

Ralph's Farm

2

Hanningfield Resr

Hounden Wood

OLD BARN LA

Lacey's Farm

Bromley Lodge

1

Hall Farm

CHURCH LA

98

A B C D E F
74 75

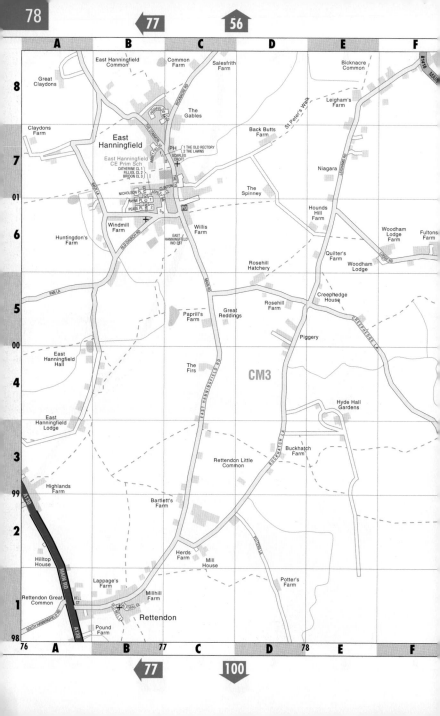

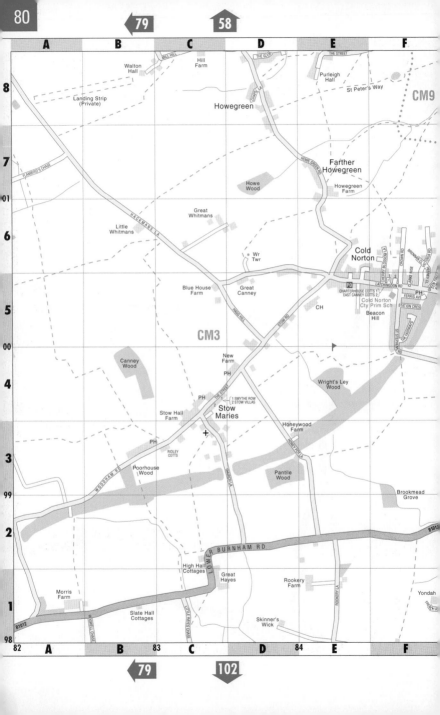

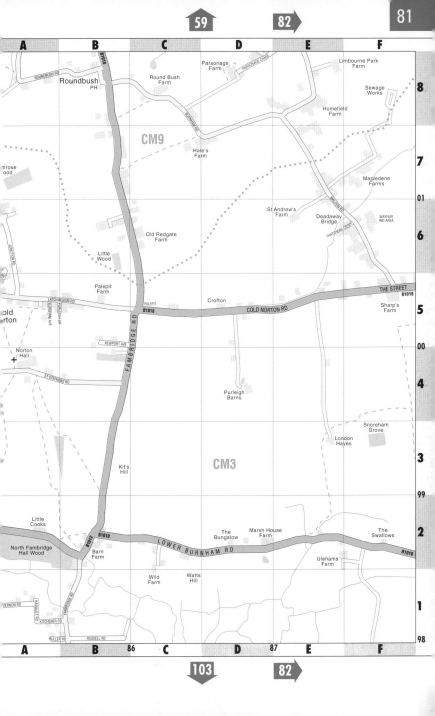

A B C D E F

ROUNDBUSH RD

Roundbush
PH

B1010

Round Bush
Farm

Parsonage
Farm

PARSONAGE CHASE

Limbourne Park
Farm

Sewage
Works

8

CM9

BURNHAM RD

Homefield
Farm

Hale's
Farm

7

nrose
ood

Mapledene
Farms

01

St Andrew's
Farm

MALDON RD

MAYFAIR
IND AREA

Deadaway
Bridge

THATCHERS CROFT

Old Redgate
Farm

6

Little
Wood

JUNCTION RD

Palepit
Farm

THE STREET

B1018

old
rton

LATCHINGDON RD

BURNHAM AVE

PURLEIGH GR

PALEPIT

B1018

Crofton

COLD NORTON RD

Sharp's
Farm

5

FAMBRIDGE RD

NEWPORT AVE

00

Norton
Hall

ST STEPHENS RD

4

Purleigh
Barns

Snoreham
Grove

London
Hayes

Kit's
Hill

CM3

3

99

Little
Cooks

B1010

The
Bungalow

Marsh House
Farm

The
Swallows

2

North Fambridge
Hall Wood

B1012

LOWER BURNHAM RD

B1010

Barn
Farm

Ulehams
Farm

VERNON RD

HANNAH RD

FAMBRIDGE RD

Wild
Farm

Watts
Hill

1

KITCHENER RD

BULLER RD

RUSSELL RD

98

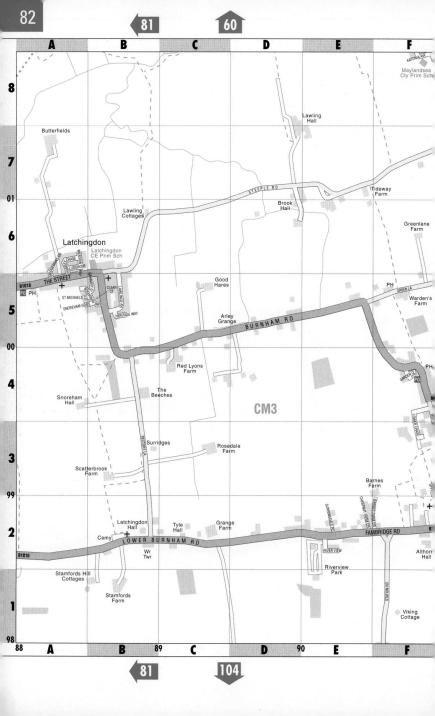

A B C D E F

8

Mayland
1 ST STEPHENS CT
2 ST JOHNS CT
3 WHITEFIELD CT

PRINCES AVE

SMITHE AVE

WHITFIELD CLOSE

DRAKE AVE

YOUNG AVE

MILL RD

MALDON RD

Lower
Farm

Ashtree
Farm

Little Ashtree
Farm

Steeple
Hill

PH

STEEPLE RD

Firth View
Farm

7

Highlands

Foxhall
Farm

01

HIGHLANDS HILL

FOXHALL RD

Bicknacre Lodge
Farm

GREEN LA

CM0

6

5

Mayland
Hall

Bovill
Uplands

Hemmells

BACK WARD HILL

Mayland
Court

CM3

00

The
Moat House

Button's
Hill

Mayland Hall
Farm Cottages

4

Button's Hill
Farm

BUTTON'S HILL

SOUTHMINSTER RD

Ewenny
Farm

B1018

Scott's
Farm

Medway
Farm

Joyce's
Farm

Dairy
Farm

3

IMMERDALE

WOODLANDS

OAKWOOD CT

DAIRY FARM RD

Petersville

OLD HEATH RD

99

Althorne

Austral
Farm

PH

Poultry
Houses

High House
Farm

2

Mansfield
Poultry
Farm

St Helier

Althorne
Lodge

THE ENDWAY

BURNHAM RD

Hill
Farm

The
Wrekin

1

Andrews
Farm

Stoke's
Hall

98

A B 92 C D 93 E F

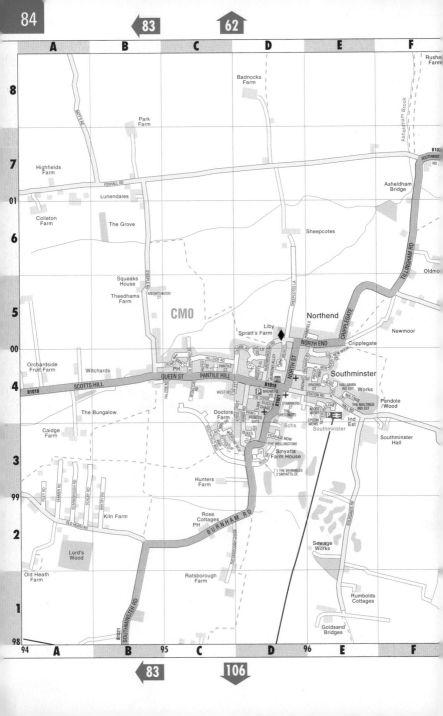

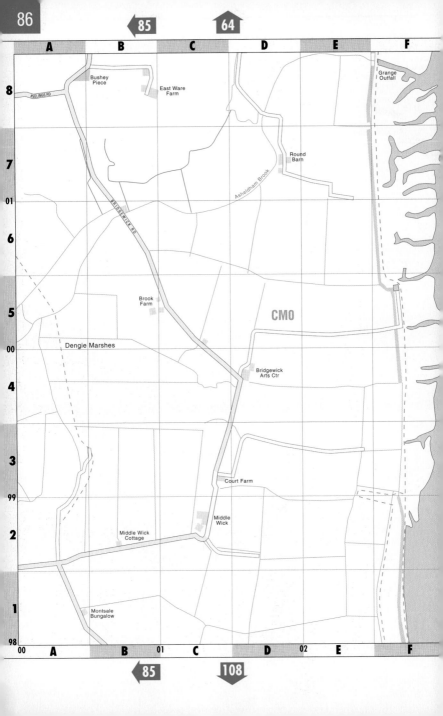

85
64

A   B   C   D   E   F

8

FEELINGS RD

Bushey
Piece

East Ware
Farm

Grange
Outfall

7

Round
Barn

Asheldham Brook

01

BRIDGEWICK RD

6

Brook
Farm

5

CM0

00

Dengie Marshes

4

Bridgewick
Arts Ctr

3

Court Farm

99

Middle
Wick

2

Middle Wick
Cottage

1

Montsale
Bungalow

98

00   A   B   01   C   D   02   E   F

85
108

Manor Farm

Weirs

PH A112
BODERY

Netherhouse Farm

Sewardstone

8

Nurseries

Barn Hill

Aldergrove Wood

MOTT ST

IG10

Blind La

Day's Farm

EN3

Luthers Farm

Woodlands Farm

Green La

Police Training Camp

UPPER HILL

PH

7

97

MARSH LA
HEREFR

MILL LA

DAWS HILL

Pick's Farm

Gilwellbury

Carrolls Farm

West Essex Golf Course

Springfield Farm

6

King George's Rear

River Lea or Lea Diversion

SEWARDSTONE RD

NORTH BANK

GREENWICH MERIDIAN

Gilwell Park

GILWELL LA

CH

Ludgate Water

Ludgate Plain

5

96

Yardley Hill

E4

Bury Farm

HORNBEAM LA

WOODMAN LA

Ludgate Plain

Cuckoo Brook

Woodman's Glade

Bury Wood

4

SEWARDSTONE GDNS
BOARDMAN AVE
ANT HILL
DEERLEAP
YARDLEY CL
YARDLEY LA

Hawkswood Sch

The Hawk Wood

Sewardstonebury

HAWKWOOD CRES
HAWKDENE
YARDLEY LA

Yardley Prim Sch

Nursery

Chingford Plain

Recreation Gd

3

LEA VALLEY RD

Albany Ct 1
RIVERSIDE Ct 2

CHELWOOD
JAMES CLOSE
MARK AVE

EPPING WAY

REDWOOD GDNS
DELLS CL

MARGARET AVE

MARK AVE
HAZELWOOD CL

Obelisk Pole Hill

ASH 1 2
FOREST VIEW
ST THERESA CT

1 DONCEL CT
2 WALSINGHAM HO
3 ST JOSEPH'S CT
4 BITTERN CT
5 MALLARD CT
6 CONNAUGHT CT
7 WOOLDEN HO

8 FAIRMEAD CT
9 LOCKHART LODGE
10 CAVENDISH CT
11 OAKWOOD CT
12 THE PLAINS
13 HADLEIGH CT
14 FOREST HO
15 MATHIESON HO

Queen Elizabeth's Hunting Lodge Mus

95

BAYTREE HO 3
STONIHILL CT 4

LOW HALL CL

REDWOOD GDNS

ENTERPRISE
SUNNYSIDE DR

CONNAUGHT AVE

Frederica Rd

Buxton Rd

Sch

FOREST APP

FOREST AVE

CH

PH

RANGER'S RD

Chingford

A1069

P

Warren Pond

2

m Girling Rear

Playing Field

WALTHAM WAY A1037

MANSFIELD HILL A112

SEYMOUR RD
SUNSET AVE

LAUREL RD

MAIDA AVE

COLLEGE GDNS

KINGS HEAD HILL

MOUNT ECHO DR

COLLEGE RD

Chingford Green

MOUNT VIEW RD

THE GREEN

THE RIDGEWAY

Mount Pleasant

WILLINGAE RD

STATION RD

Liby

Sch

THE RISE

Sch

Warren Pond

CHINGFORD

SCH TREE GLADE

OAKWOOD SCH

1

LAWRENCE'S HILL

Chingford Sch

THE RIDGEWAY

KINGS RD A110

BALCONE RD

FAVERSHAM AVE

LITTLE LA

VALANCE

THE COPSE

94

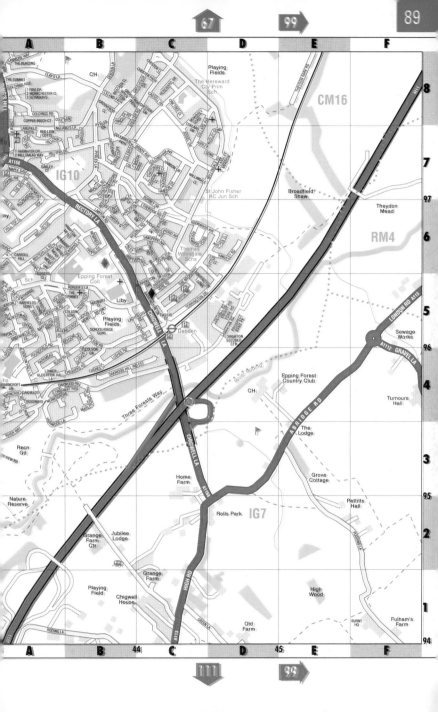

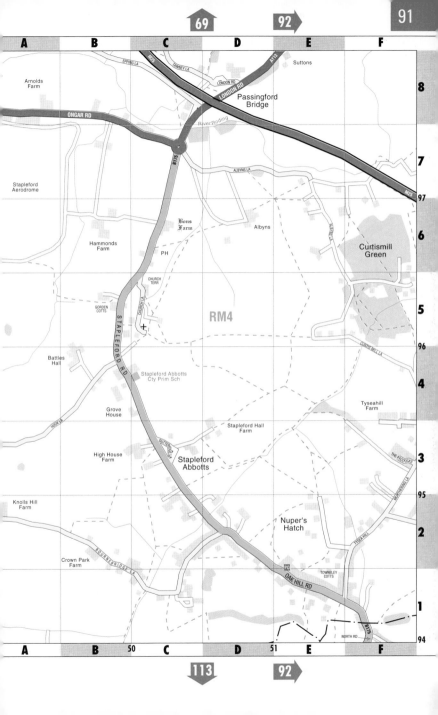

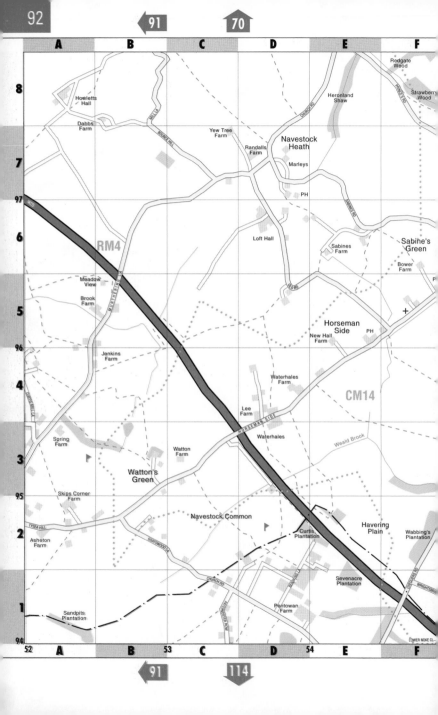

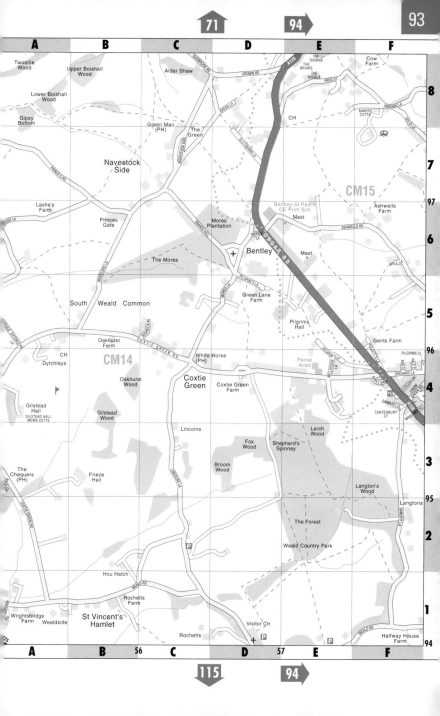

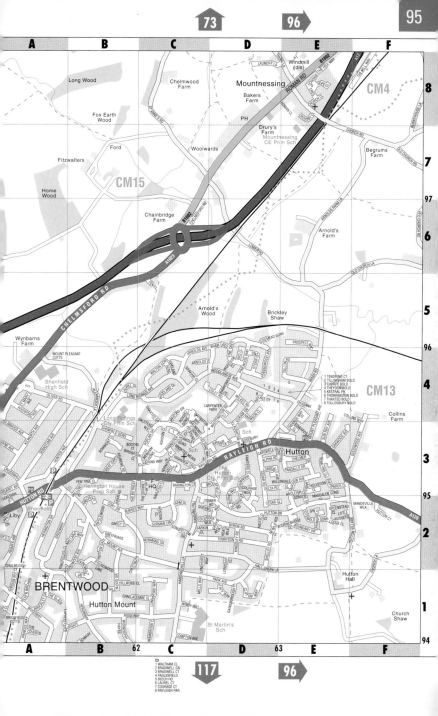

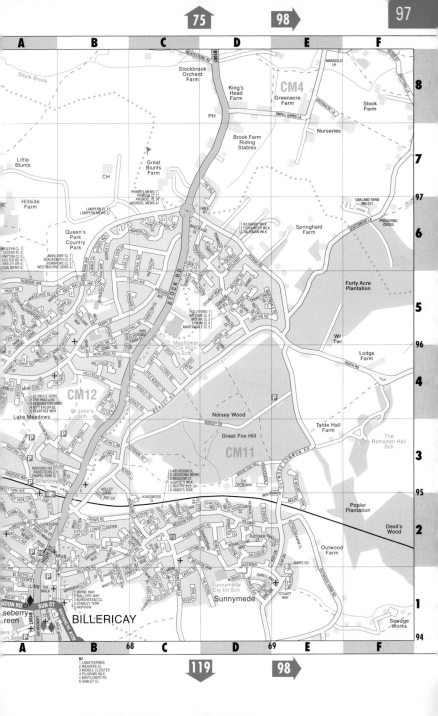

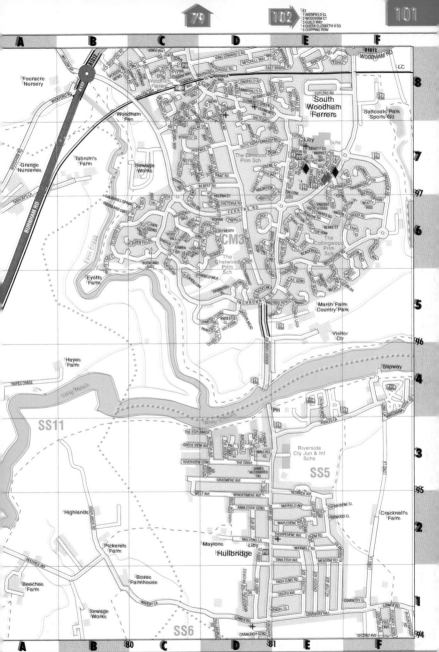

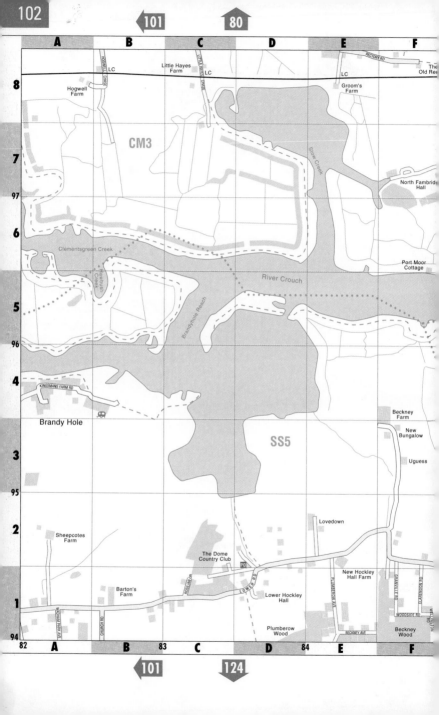

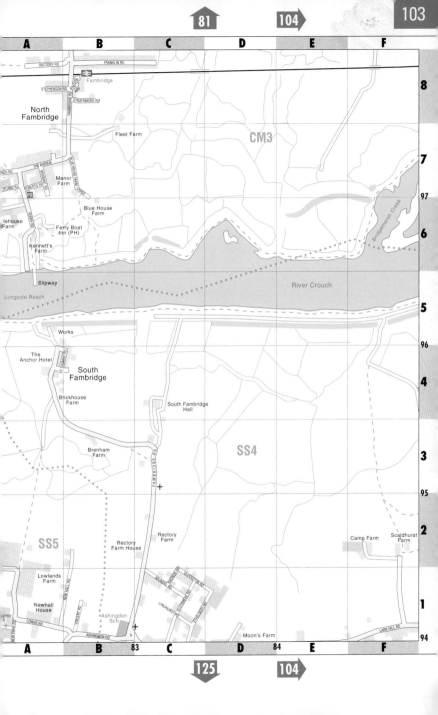

A   B   C   D   E   F

8

CM3

← STATION RD
Althorne   LC
LC

BRIDGEMARSH LA

Althorne Creek

7
Bridgemarsh Creek

97
Bridgemarsh
Island

6

Shortpole Reach

Raypits Reach

Landsend
Point

River Crouch   Easter Reach

5

96
Upper Raypits
Farm

4
Old Fleet

3
SS4

Pudsey Hall

Market
Hill

95
Butts Hill

2
Bolt Hall

Beacon Hill   New Hall
Farm

Canewdon Hall
Farm

BUTTS PADDOCK

CANEWDON HALL

KETTS MEAD

GATE CL

ALDERTON TWY

CROUCH VIEW
VILLAS

LAMBOURNE HALL RD

LARKHILL AVE

CHESTNUT
PATH

HIGH ST
CHURCH

Canewdon
Prim Sch

ORCHARD
BGLWS

PUDSEY HALL LA

ASH LDN
WILLOW WLK
CHASE
ROWAN WAY

ANCHOR
PAR

GARDENERS LA

1
LARK HILL RD

GREEN
WLK

ANCHOR LA

ANCHOR LANE
COTTS

Gardeners

White House
Farm

SCOTTS HALL RD

Canewdon

94

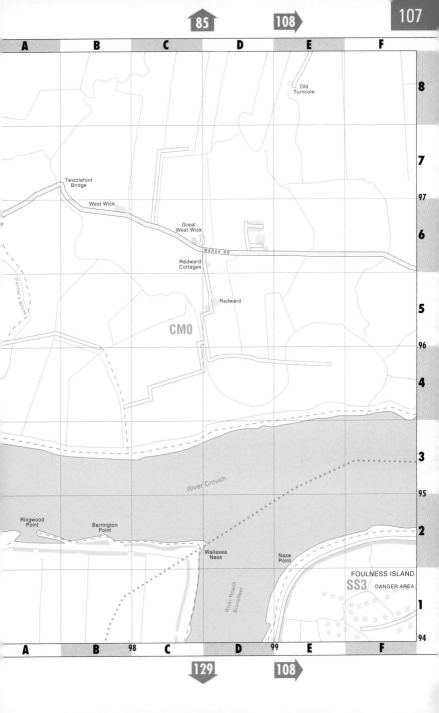

A B C D E F

8

7

97

6

Old Turncole

Twizzlefoot Bridge

West Wick

Great West Wick

MARSH RD

Redward Cottages

Redward

Parmel's Brook

CM0

5

96

4

River Crouch

3

95

Ringwood Point

Barrington Point

Wallasea Ness

Nase Point

FOULNESS ISLAND

SS3 DANGER AREA

2

River Roach Brankfleet

1

94

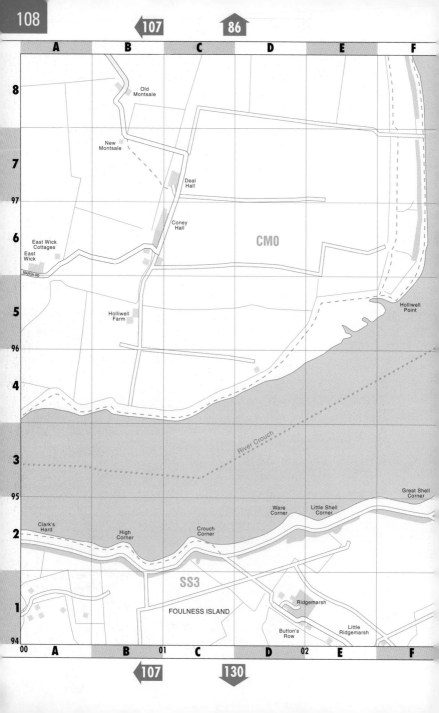

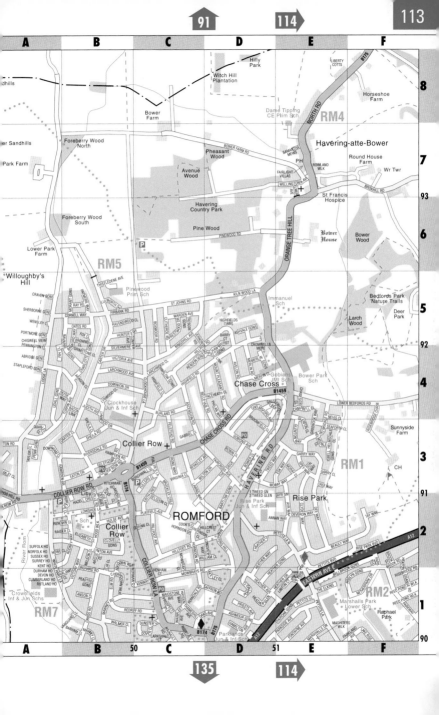

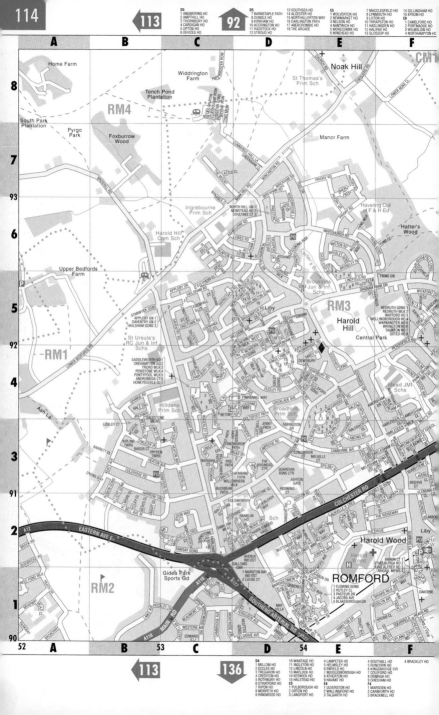

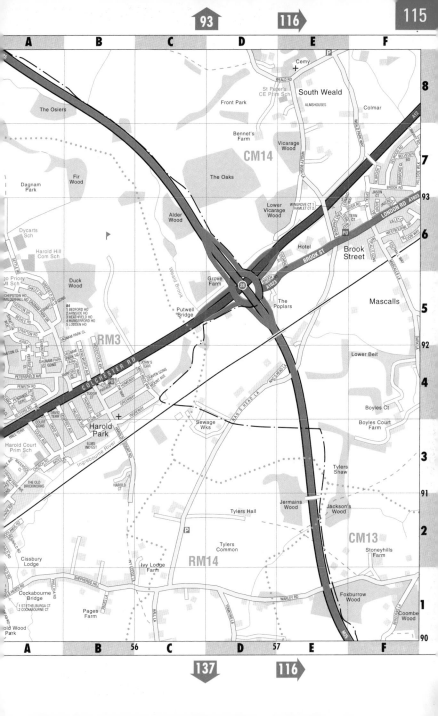

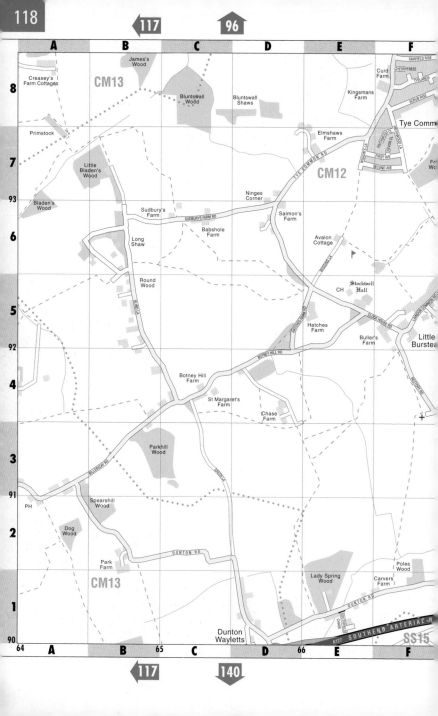

CM13

James's Wood

Creasey's Farm Cottages

CM13

Bluntswall Wood

Bluntswall Shaws

8

Primstock

Little Bladen's Wood

7

93

Bladen's Wood

Sudbury's Farm

SUDBURYS FARM RD

Ninges Corner

Salmon's Farm

Babshole Farm

Long Shaw

6

Round Wood

Avalon Cottage

Stockwell Hall

CH

Curd Farm

Cherrytrees

Kingsmans Farm

Elmshaws Farm

CM12

Tye Comm

FAIRFIELD RISE

TYELANDS

SCRUB RISE

FIRST AVE

SECOND AVE

TYE COMMON RD

WIGGINS LA

WIDDINGS LA

5

92

Hatches Farm

Buller's Farm

Buck Louse RD

Little Burstea

LANGDON COMMON RD

Botney Hill RD

Botney Hill Farm

4

St Margaret's Farm

Chase Farm

HATCHES LANE RD

BING LA

Parkhill Wood

3

91

PH

Spearshill Wood

BILLERICAY RD

Dog Wood

2

GREEN LA

Park Farm

DUNTON RD

CM13

Lady Spring Wood

Carvers Farm

Poles Wood

DUNTON RD

1

90

Dunton Wayletts

SOUTHEND ARTERIAL R

A127

SOUTHEND CHASE

SS15

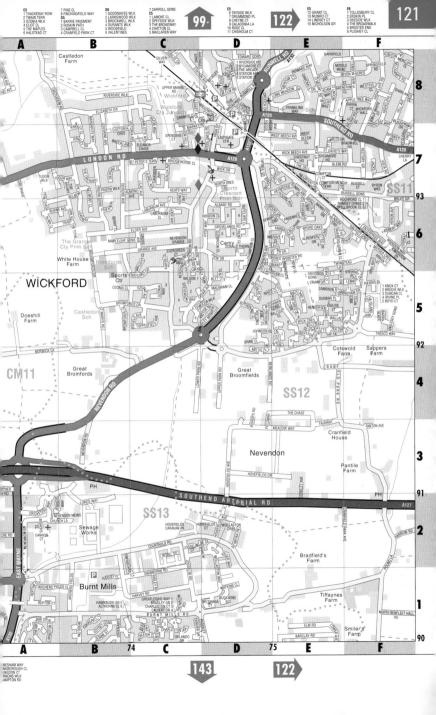

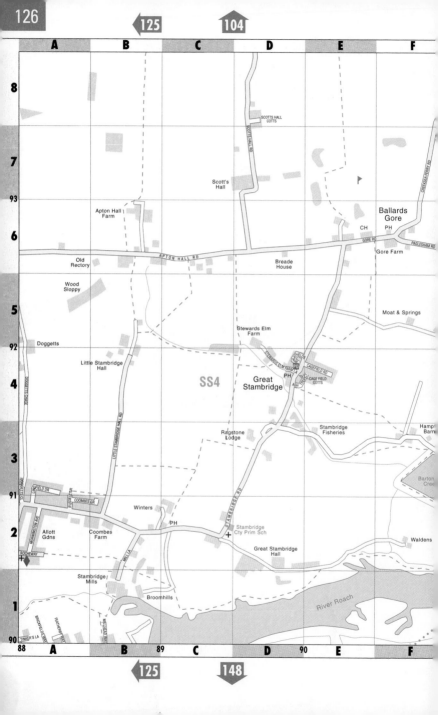

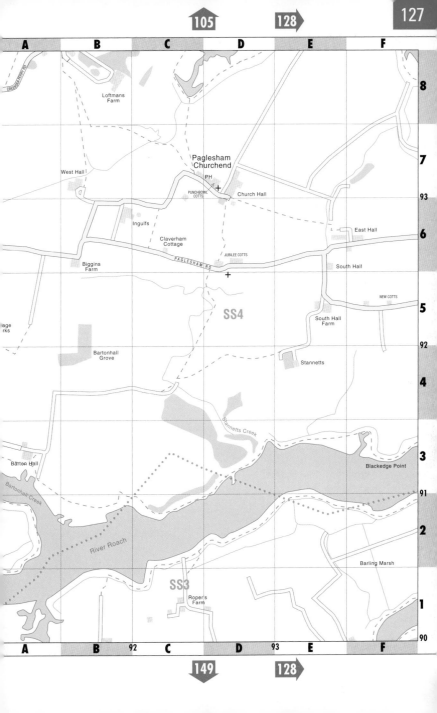

8

Loftmans
Farm

7

West Hall

Paglesham
Churchend

PH

93

Church Hall

PUNCHBOWL
COTTS

Ingulfs

East Hall

Claverham
Cottage

6

PAGLESHAM RD

Biggins
Farm

JUBILEE COTTS

South Hall

SS4

NEW COTTS

5

South Hall
Farm

92

Bartonhall
Grove

Stannetts

age
rks

4

Stannetts Creek

Barton Hall

3

Blackedge Point

Bartonhall Creek

91

River Roach

2

Barling Marsh

SS3

Roper's
Farm

1

90

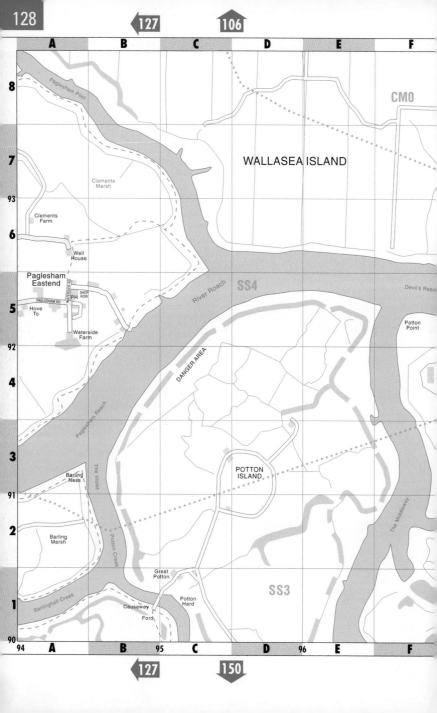

8 Paglesham Pool

CM0

7 WALLASEA ISLAND

Clements
Marsh

93

Clements
Farm

6 Well
House

Paglesham
Eastend

SS4

Devil's Reach

WATERSIDE RD
SHOP
ROW
PH

Potton
Point

5 PAGLESHAM RD

Hove
To

Waterside
Farm

River Roach

92 DANGER AREA

4 Paglesham Reach

3 Barling
Ness POTTON
ISLAND

91 The Violet

2 Barling
Marsh Potton Creek

The Middleway

SS3

Great
Potton

1 Potton
Hard

Barlinghall Creek Causeway

Ford

90
94 A B 95 C D 96 E F

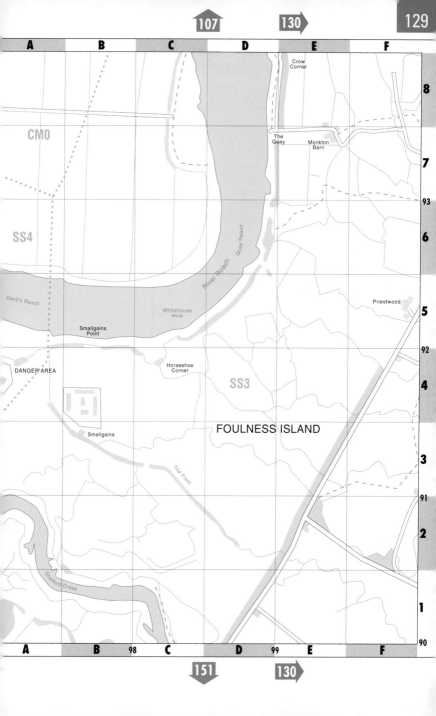

8

7

93

6

5

92

4

91

3

2

1

90

CMO

SS4

Devil's Reach

DANGER AREA

Smallgains
Point

Smallgains

Whitehouse
Hole

The Fleet

Shelford Creek

Crow
Corner

The
Quay

Monkton
Barn

River Roach

Quay Reach

Horseshoe
Corner

SS3

Priestwood

FOULNESS ISLAND

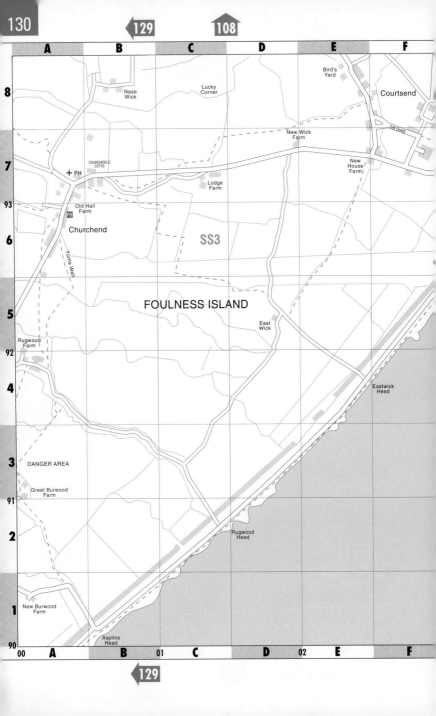

108

| A | B | C | D | E | F |

River Crouch

8

Foulness Point

7

95

East
Newlands

The Drift
(dis)

6

SS3

5

DANGER AREA

94

4

Northern
Corner

3

93

Fisherman's
Head

2

1

92

| A | B | 04 | C | D | 05 | E | F |

130

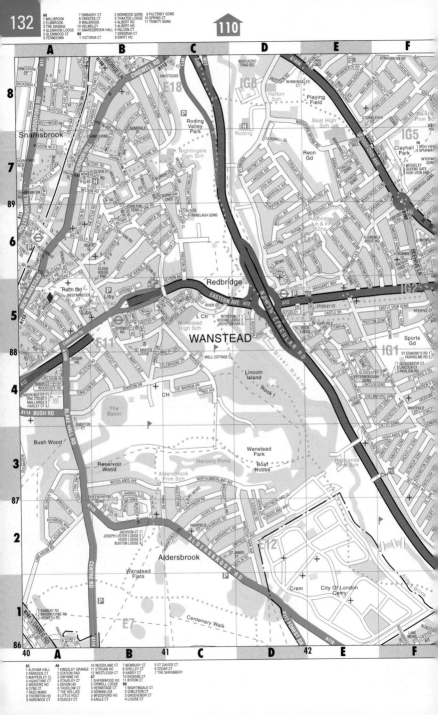

110

Map Labels

Row 8
KINGSPARK CT
BROADWALK
CLARENDON RD
HAYSTOCK CT
BEECHWOOD
Snaresbrook
MEADOW WLK
HAYSTOCKS
E18
GEORGE LA
CHIGWELL RD A113
WOODFORD TRAD EST
IG8
WINNINGALES CT
Hatton Sch
STRADBROKE GR
Playing Field

Row 7
HERMITAGE
Snaresbrook
EAST HOUSE
Nightingale Prim Sch
Roding Valley Park
Beal High Sch
CARSWELL CL
Recn Gd
IG5
Clayhall Park
HIGH VIEW
QUEENS GATE
HIGH VIEW PARK

Row 89/6
Snaresbrook
WELLESLEY
KEATS
EATON RISE
RANELAGH GDNS
CARLTON TERR
BURNHAM CRES
CLOCK HOUSE PAR

Row 5
Recn Gd
WESTMINSTER
Wanstead Liby
Wanstead High Sch
Redbridge
EASTERN AVE A12
Redbridge
MARGARET WAY
ROYSTON CT
RODING LODGE 2
ROYSTON PAR 3
STUDLEY CT
CASTLE VIEW GDNS
BEEHIVE CT
Sports Gd
IG1

Row 88
E11
ST MARY'S LODGE
COLEBROOKE DR
WELL COTTAGE CL
WANSTEAD
CARLISLE
ST EDMUND'S RD 1
FAIRHOLME RD 2
1 GLOUCESTER CT
2 LINCOLN CT
3 PAVILION RD

Row 4
NADIR CT
WOODCOTE RD
TENNERÉE CT 1
OAK COTTS 2
MALLARDS 3
HARLEY CT 4
A12
A114 BUSH RD
OVERTON DR
THE WARREN DR
PINE AVE
Lincoln Island
Rook I
River Roding
CHELMSFORD GDNS
ST ANDREW'S
WHITFIELD

Row 3
Bush Wood
Reservoir Wood
QUEENSWOOD GDNS
Heronry Pond
Wanstead Park
Boat House
Highlands Prim Sch
CH

Row 87/2
ST GABRIEL S CL
SAL CRES
Aldersbrook Prim Sch
WOODLANDS AVE
NORTHUMBERLAND AVE
PARK RD
DOVER RD
HIGHFIELD
ST MARGARETS RD
ALDERSBROOK RD
E12

Row 2
JACKSON CT 1
JOSEPH LISTER LODGE 2
WOOD LODGE 3
BUXTON LODGE 4
Aldersbrook
Wanstead Flats
ST JAMES
Crem
City Of London Cemy

Row 1/86
1 RAMSAY RD
2 BROXBOURNE RD
3 HESKETH RD
E7
Centenary Walk
A116 FOREST DR

40   A   B   41   C   D   42   E   F

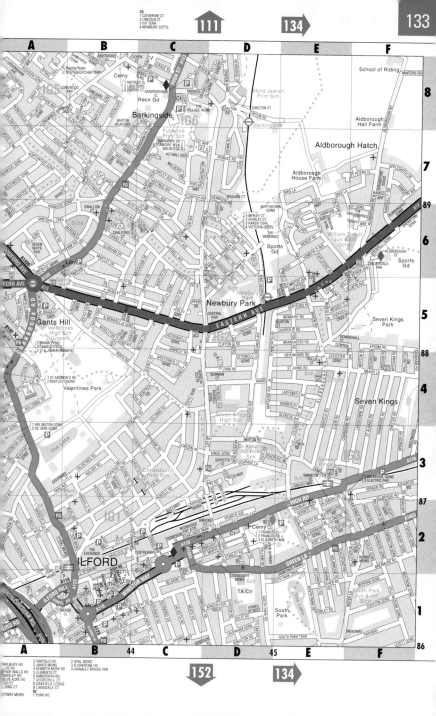

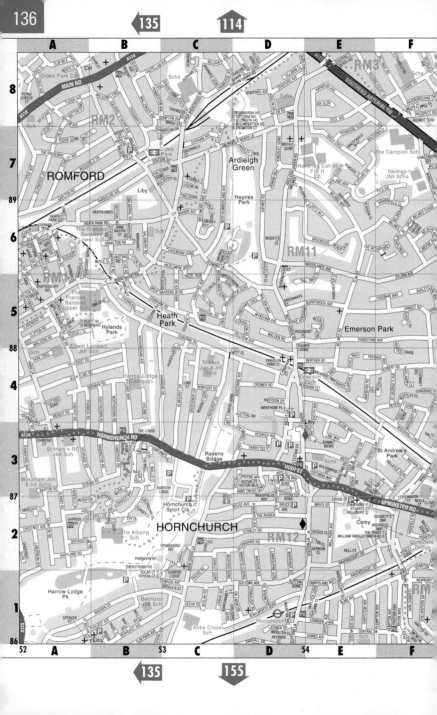

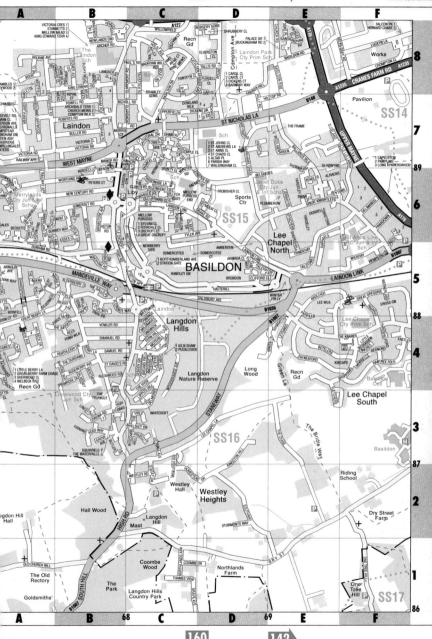

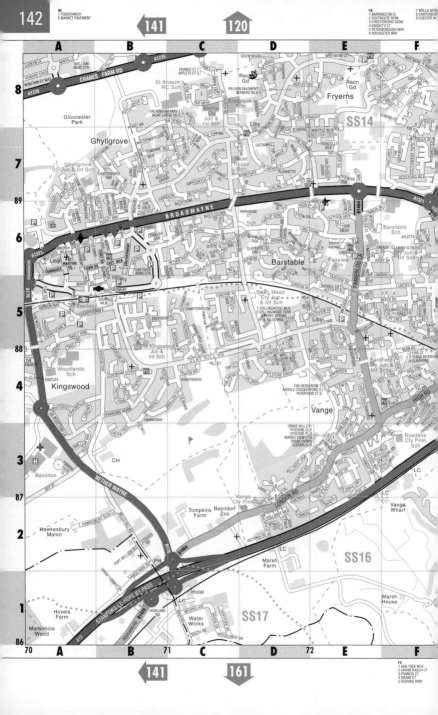

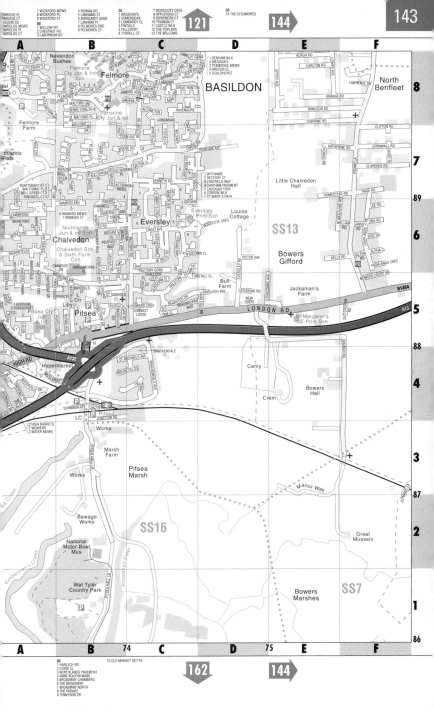

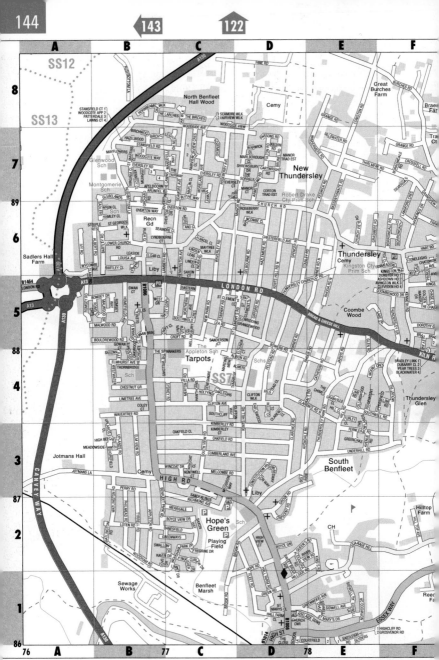

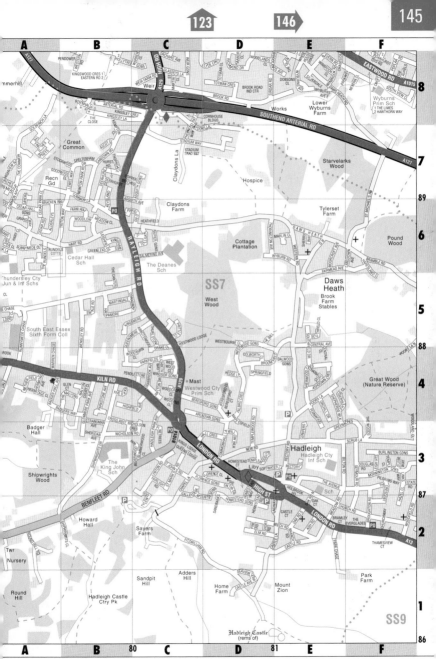

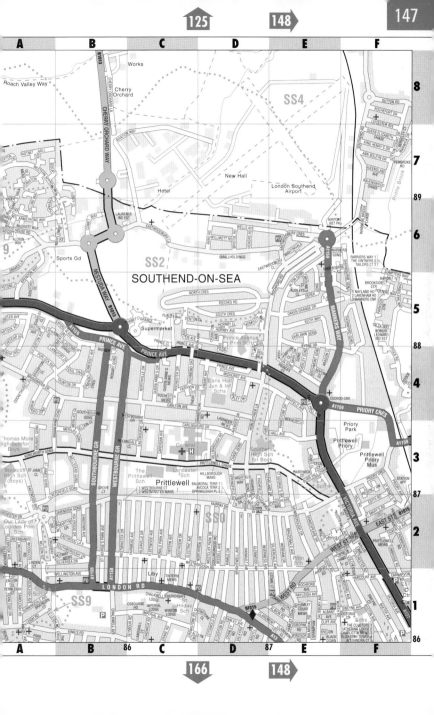

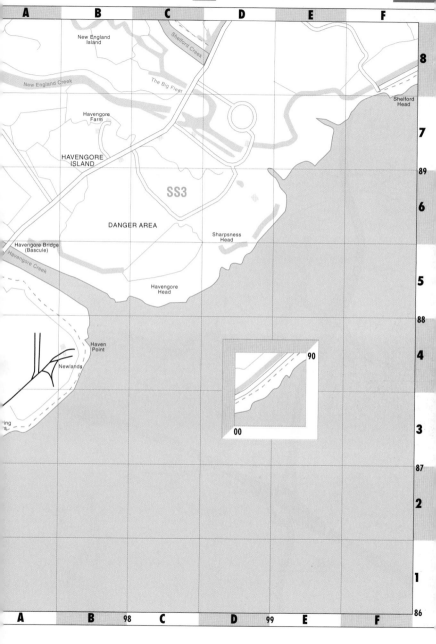

A   B   C   D   E   F

8

Shelford Creek

New England
Island

Shelford
Head

New England Creek

The Big Fleet

7

Havengore
Farm

89

HAVENGORE
ISLAND

SS3

6

DANGER AREA

Sharpsness
Head

Havengore Bridge
(Bascule)

5

Havengore Creek

Havengore
Head

88

Haven
Point

4

90

Newlands

ring
s

00

3

87

2

87

1

86

A   B   98   C   D   99   E   F

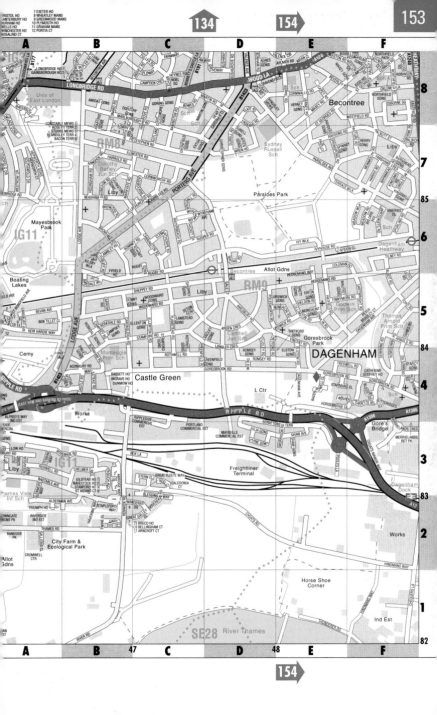

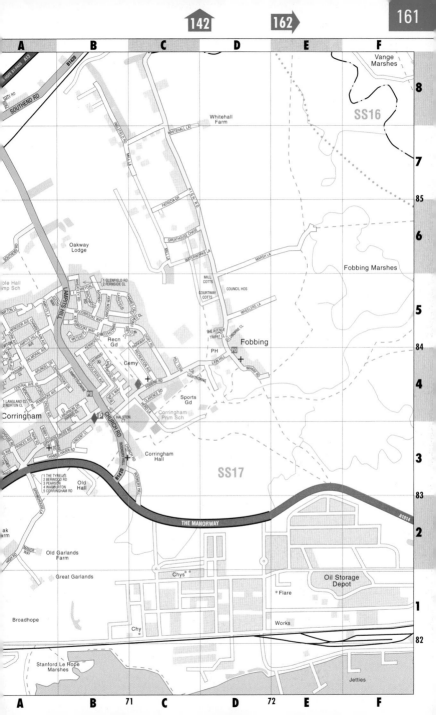

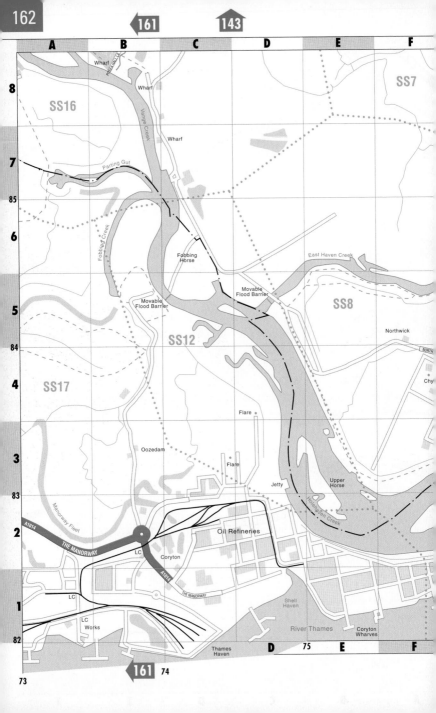

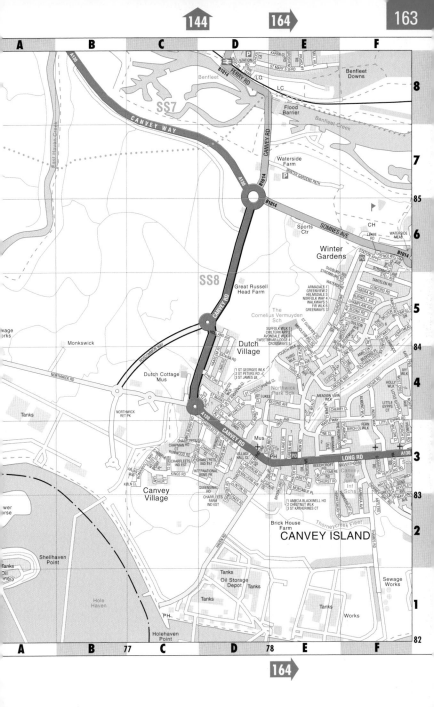

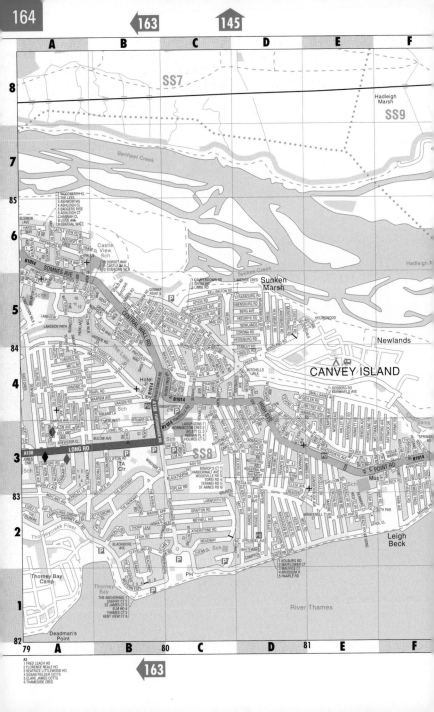

A B C D E F

8

SS7

Hadleigh
Marsh

SS9

7

Benfleet Creek

85

1 WOODBERRY CL
2 THE LEES
3 ASHWORTHS
4 ASHLEIGH CL
5 BADGERS RISE
6 ASHLEIGH CT
7 HANNAH CL
8 LEIGE AVE
9 CENTRAL WAY

6

ELSINOR
AVE
HARDYS
WAY

Castle
View
Sch

10 DORSET WAY
11 CASTLE WLK
12 STAFFORD WLK

SOMNES AVE

B1014

Tewkes Creek

Sunken
Marsh

Hadleigh F

1 CAMPERDOWN RD
2 GEESLER
3 LRRIE

KELLINGTON RD

5

CENTRAL WAY RD

STRASBOURG RD
ABENBURG RD
BERG AVE
HEESWYK RD
NEWLANDS RD
CORONA RD
HEIDEBURG RD

Lakeside Cres

HOLMSWOOD

Newlands

LAKEVIEW

LAKESIDE PATH

84

The Lane

STANLEY RD
HINDLES RD

CANVEY ISLAND

EAST CRES

TONGRES RD

MELZ RD

Hotel
Lib

MITCHELLS
WLK

B1014

4

URMOND RD

WAAREM AVE

VAAGEN RD

BRAINDON RD

1 ROSBERG RD
2 BRAINVELD AVE

SMALL GAINS AVE

HIGH ST

WAMBURG RD

A130
JONES
CNR

LONG RD

KNIGHTSWICK
CTR

B1014

LARUPGDNS 1
MORNINGTON CRES 2
AYLETT CL 3
KRESGON PL 4
HOLMES CT 5

Sch

3

STAFFORD RD

TA
Ctr

OAK RD

ELM RD

SS8

BISHOP'S CT 1
VANDERWALT AVE 2
WOODVILLE RD 3
TORSI RD 4
TERAMO RD 5
ST ANNES RD 6

STELLA
MARIS

Mus

S POINT RD

B1014

BLACKTHORNE

POPLAR RD

83

ESSEX WAY
THE
FREMNES

BAY CL

LANBOURNE
CHICHESTER

TILBURY

ASH RD

LABOURTH RD

GRAFTON RD

MEYNELL AVE

DELDER AVE

SHELDON RD

Sch

SOUTH PAR

2

Thorneycreek Fleet

BLACKMORE
AVE

THORP LEAS

HOWA CL

LEIGH RD

ATHERSTONE RD

MEADWAY

ODENS CL

Sch

SPRUNDEL AVE

WHITEWAYS

COMPTON

Leigh
Beck

ATHOL CL

1 KOLBURG RD
2 MAYFLOWER CT
3 MAURICE CT
4 BRUSSUM R
5 HAARLE RD

Thorney Bay
Camp

Thorney
Bay

CLEVELAND RD

PH

1

THE ANCHORAGE 1
CHERRY CT 2
ST JAMES CT 3
ELM HO 4
THAMES CT 5
KENT VIEW CT 6

River Thames

82

Deadman's
Point

79 A B 80 C D 81 E F

163

A3
1 FRED LEACH HO
2 FLORENCE NEALE HO
3 BEATRICE LITTLEWOOD HO
4 SUSAN FIELDER COTTS
5 CLARE JAMES COTTS
6 THAMESIDE CRES

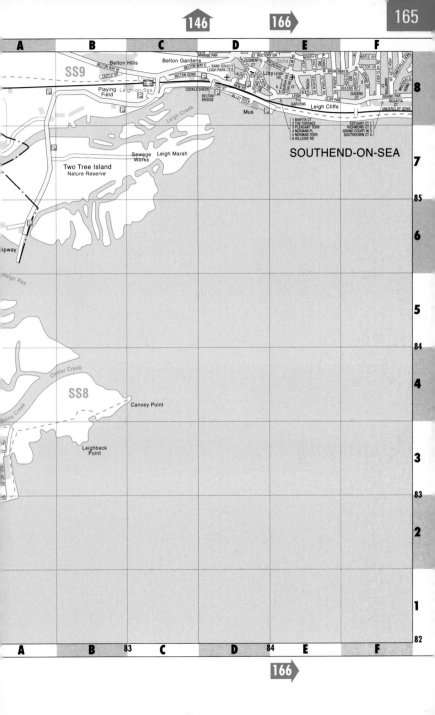

A   B   C   D   E   F

SS9

Belton Hills

Belton Gardens

MARINE PAR

ST. RECTORY GR.

MAPLE AVE

BELTON WAY W
BELTON WAY E
CASTLE DR.
BELTON GDNS.

Playing Field   Leigh-on-Sea

CLEMENT'S CT
BROADWAY W
SANS SOUCI 1
LEIGH PARK CT 2
LAUREL
NEW RD
HIGH ST
BELTON BRIDGE
ALLEY DOCK
COCKLE SHEDS
Mus

NORTH ST
WEST ST
EAST ST
ALEXANDRA
VICTORIA RD
BROADWAY
HORNBY
SEAVEN
CLIFF PAR
THE GARDENS
QUEENS
Liby   Leigh Ho.
Schs
VICTOR DR
HIGH CLIFF DR
COMPMPELLE GDNS
CLIFF TOWN RD
QUEENS RD
Leigh Cliffs

GRAND PAR
REGATTA CT
GRAND CT
UNDERCLIFF GDNS
ESTUARY CT 1
RICHMOND CT 2
GRAND COURT W 3
SOUTHDOWN CT 4

1 BARYTA CT
2 THE TERRACE
3 PLEASANT TERR
4 NORMAN PL
5 NORMAN TERR
6 HILLSIDE RD

SOUTHEND-ON-SEA

Leigh Creek

Sewage Works   Leigh Marsh

Two Tree Island
Nature Reserve

ipway

leigh Ray

Oyster Creek

SS8

Canvey Point

ains Creek

Leighbeck Point

85

7

84

6

5

84

4

83

3

83

2

1

82

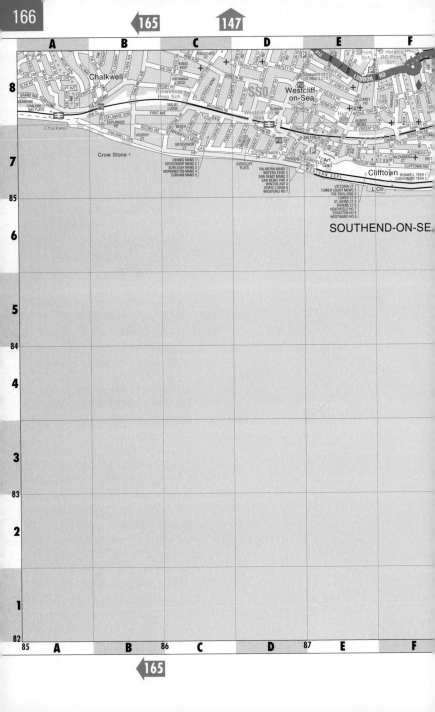

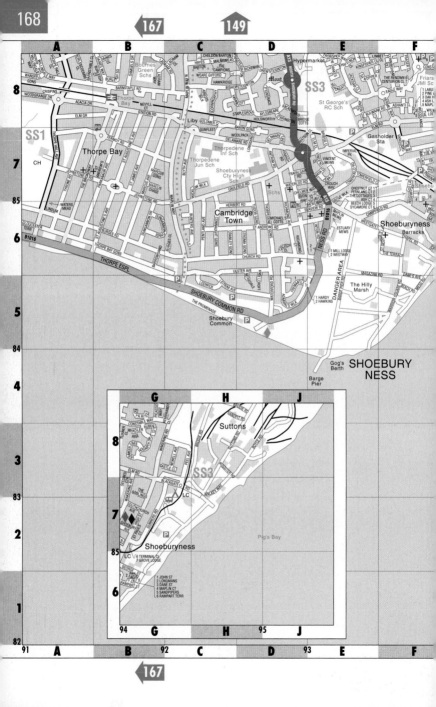

Map labels

A **B** **C** **D** **E** **F**

LAMSON RD
LC
P
BUCKLEY'S YD
FERRY LA
ELIZABETH RD
FREEMAN
FREDA PK
BENNETT RD
BROOKWAY
RUSHDEN DR
JUNTLAND
GERVE
B1335
WANTZ LA
LAMB DELA
DERI AVE
The Chafford Sch

A1306

8

SOUTH HALL DR
MANGSTEAD
EASTWOOD DR

Brady Prim Sch

South Hall Farm

Southall Bridge

East Hall Farm

WENNINGTON RD

EAST HALL LA

LAMBOURNE LA

NEW RD

7

A13

NEW COTTAGES

CHURCH LA END CLOSE

Wennington Hall Farm

The Willows

81

Rainham Marshes

LAUNDRY COTTS
MARINE COTTS
KENT VIEW

WENNINGTON GN
Wennington

B1335

PH

RM13

SANDY L

6

Silt Lagoons

A13

5

Wennington Marshes

BLYTHE WAY
PURFI IND

80

COLDHARBOUR LA

RM15

PURFLEET BY PASS

4

Purfleet Rifle Ranges

3

Aveley Marshes

DA8

79

FREIGHTMASTER EST

RM19

MARINE
MARGET RD

2

River Thames

RAPIER CL

Erith Rands

TANK HILL

LONDON RD PURFLEET

1

Crayford Ness

DARENT IND PK

LANDSAI WAY
DARENT IND RD

78

DAYTON DR

52 **A** **B** 53 **C** **D** 54 **E** **F**

156 172

A B C D E F

Bretts Farm

PH

Moor Hall

GDNS

Kenningtons City Jun Sch

PINFOLDS
WAYMANS
MERESMANS
HAYWARDS
FRANKLINS

Belhus Park

CH

Oak Wood

Long Pond

ERRUD DR

Ash Plantation

LOMAN PATH

Dilkes Prim Sch

GATEHOPE DR

SHANNON WAY

GDNS

NETHAN DR

Aveley Comp Sch

PARK LA

Sports Gd

GROVES CL

FULBROOK

SANDY LA

AVELEY BY-PASS

RM15

ST PAUL

STIFFORD RD

B1335

Aveley

ST MICHAELS

MARTIN RD

PARK VIEW

KELLY HO

DACRE CRES

ELM RD

BROOME PL COMPLEX

STANFORD RD

Hangman's Wood

TOPLANDS AVE

MAN HO

HESTER CL

BROOME PL

STIFFORD RD

LOWLAN

MANOR CL S

Ilby

THE ROWANS

THE SYCAMORES

NEW MALTINGS

AVELEY CLOSE

Aveley Cty Jun Sch

Oak Wood

Ponds Farm

PURFLEET RD

ARNHEM AVE

LISBON ROW

RM16

MYRTLE CFT

CHURCH VW

Thurrock Management Ctr

CRESCENT

LOVE LA

KENT PL

CHU CRES

HOLT TERR

LONDON RD

Sports Gd

BEVIN HO 1
THE PARADE 2
LEEHOLM HO 3

CRESCENT WLK

Fann's Farm

RM LA

M25

Oak Wood

LC

THE CARAVAN SITE

Causeway Bridge

Thurrock Service Area

WEST THURROCK WAY

Mar Dyke

A282

A1306

B186

TANK HILL RD

A1090

WATERLL

CORNWALL GATE

Watt's Wood

CARTEL CL

Broomhill

A1306

ARTERIAL ROAD PURFLEET

TANK LA

THE QUADRANT

BAILEY CL

DABURN

TUNNEL EST

Purfleet Cty Prim Sch

WOOD AVE

NORTH RD

BANNIS

CENTRAL AVE

1 CRUSADER CL
2 GARRISON PARK

Purfleet

RM19

PURFLEET BY-PASS

STONEHOUSE LA

RM20

HIGH ST

Ind Est

ROTARY WAY

A1090

Dolphin Motorway Est

WESTERN AVE

Purfleet

Beacon Hill

CON HILL

OAKHILL RD

High House

JOSLIN RD

A282

EASTERN AVE

THE GLADE BSNS CTR

LC

A1090

A B 56 C D 57 E F

B1
1 RIVERVIEW TERR
2 SUSSEX TERR
3 SOUTHLAND TERR
4 DUNCOMBE CT
5 HEBERDEN CT
6 WINGROVE DR
7 HOWBURGH CT
8 TRAYFORD CT
9 STORAS CT
10 SAWSTON CT
11 KYRKLY CT
12 BRADFIELD CT
13 RIVERVIEW FLATS
14 WROXALL CT
15 RODKLEY CT
16 DUNNOSE CT
17 BRANSTONE CT
18 SHORWELL CT
19 BRIGHSTONE CT
20 BONCHURCH CT

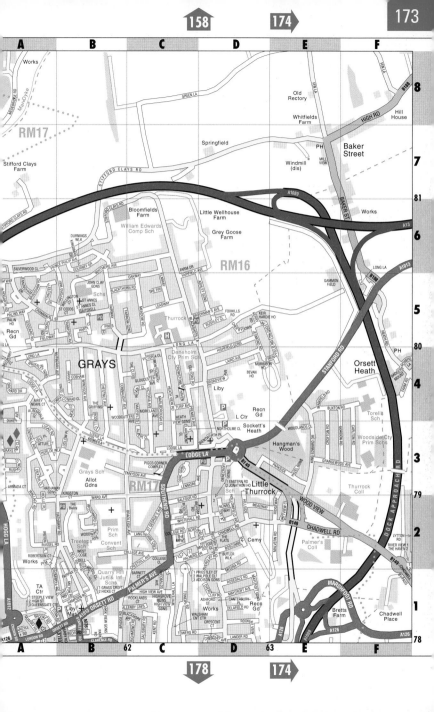

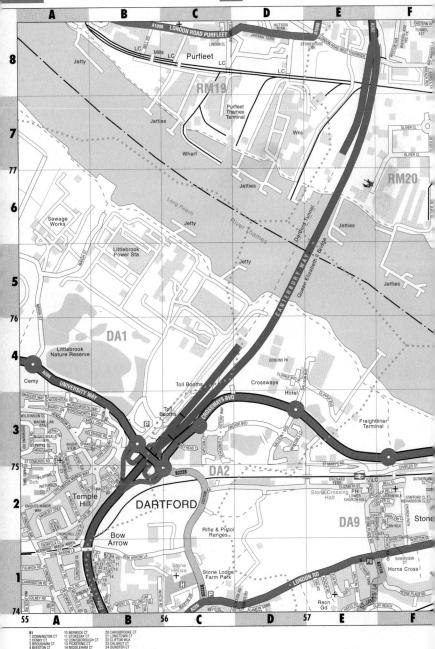

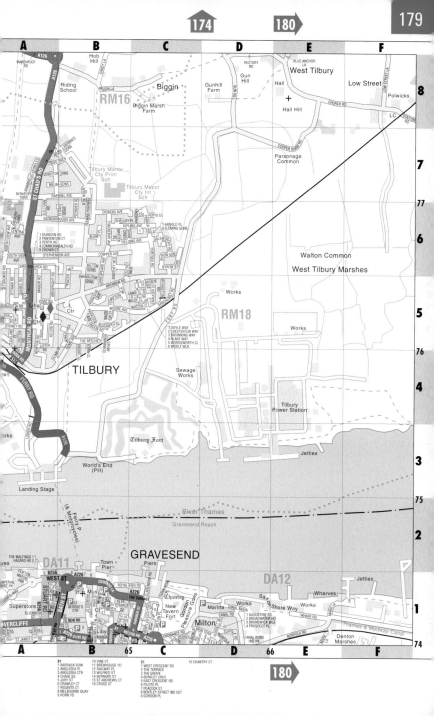

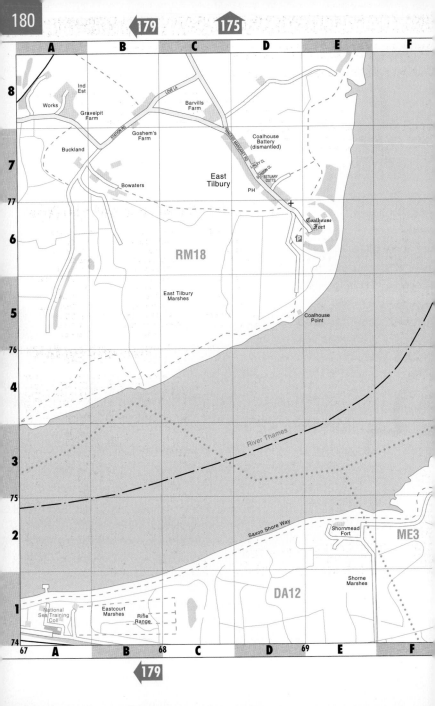

Street names are listed alphabetically and show the locality, the Postcode District, the page number and a reference to the square in which the name falls on the map page

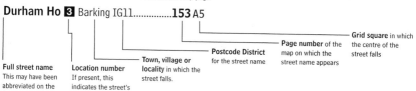

Durham Ho **3** Barking IG11...............**153** A5

Grid square in which the centre of the street falls

Page number of the map on which the street name appears

Postcode District for the street name

Town, village or locality in which the street falls.

Location number If present, this indicates the street's position on a congested area of the map instead of the name

Full street name This may have been abbreviated on the map

Abbreviations used in the index

App **Approach**	Cl **Close**	Espl **Esplanade**	Mans **Mansions**	Rdbt **Roundabout**
Arc **Arcade**	Comm **Common**	Est **Estate**	Mdw **Meadow**	S **South**
Ave **Avenue**	Cnr **Corner**	Gdns **Gardens**	N **North**	Sq **Square**
Bvd **Boulevard**	Cotts **Cottages**	Gn **Green**	Orch **Orchard**	Strs **Stairs**
Bldgs **Buildings**	Ct **Court**	Gr **Grove**	Par **Parade**	Stps **Steps**
Bsns Pk **Business Park**	Ctyd **Courtyard**	Hts **Heights**	Pas **Passage**	St **Street, Saint**
Bsns Ctr **Business Centre**	Cres **Crescent**	Ho **House**	Pl **Place**	Terr **Terrace**
Bglws **Bungalows**	Dr **Drive**	Ind Est **Industrial**	Prec **Precinct**	Tk **Track**
Cswy **Causeway**	Dro **Drove**	**Estate**	Prom **Promenade**	Trad **Trading Est**
Ctr **Centre**	E **East**	Intc **Interchange**	Ret Pk **Retail Park**	Wlk **Walk**
Circ **Circle**	Emb **Embankment**	Junc **Junction**	Rd **Road**	W **West**
Cir **Circus**	Ent **Enterprise**	La **Lane**		Yd **Yard**

Town and village index

A

Aalten Ave SS8 164 F3
Abberton IG8 110 C5
Abberton Wlk RM13 154 F4
Abbess Cl CM1 31 E2
Abbey Cl Hullbridge SS5 101 D2
Romford RM1 136 A5
Abbey Cres DA17 169 A2
Abbey Ct EN9 65 B5
Abbey Dale Cl CM17 24 C7
Abbey Fields CM3 78 B7
Abbey Mead Ind Est EN9 65 C5
Abbey Park Ind Est IG11 152 C4
Abbey Rd Barking IG11 152 B4
Barking IG11 152 C3
Billericay CM12 96 F1
Greenhithe DA9 177 C2
Hullbridge SS5 101 D1
Ilford IG2 133 D6
Abbey Turning CM9 36 D4
Abbey Wood La RM13 155 D3
Abbeyview EN9 65 C6
Abbots Cl Brentwood CM15 95 A1
Rainham RM13 155 C3
Abbots Ct SS15 119 E1
Abbots Hall Cty Jun & Inf Sch SS17 160 E3
Abbots Ride CM11 97 C2
Abbots Wlk SS3 168 C8
Abbotsford Gdns IG8 110 A3
Abbotsford Rd IG3 134 B2
Abbotsleigh Rd CM3 101 E7
Abbotsweld CM18 23 D5
Abbotsweld Cty Prim Sch CM18 23 D6
Abbotswood SS7 145 C5
Abbotswood Gdns
Ilford IG5 133 A8
Redbridge IG5 132 F8
Abbotts Cl Chelmsford CM2 32 D3
Romford RM7 135 B8
Southend-on-S SS9 146 E5
Abbotts Cres E4 109 D6
Abbotts Ct RM3 114 F2
Abbotts Dr
Stanford-le-H SS17 160 D2
Waltham Abbey EN9 66 A6
Abbotts Hall Chase SS17 160 E2
Abbotts Rise SG12 8 D4
Abbotts Way SG12 8 D4
Abbs Cross Gdns RM12 136 D3
Abbs Cross La RM12 136 C2
Abbs Cross Sch RM12 136 C1
Abell Way CM2 33 B4
Abenberg Way CM13 117 B8
Abensburg Rd SS8 164 D5
Abercorn Gdns RM6 134 B5
Abercorn Ho CM3 33 E8
Abercrombie Ho 17 RM3 114 D5
Abercrombie Way CM18 23 C6
Aberdeen Gdns SS9 146 A2
Aberdour Rd IG3 134 B2
Abigail Ct CM5 49 A5
Abigail Mews RM3 114 F1
Abingdon Ct 3 SS13 121 A1
Abinger Cl IG11 153 A8
Abington Ct RM14 137 C3
Abreys SS7 145 A7
Abridge Gdns RM5 113 A4
Abridge Rd Chigwell IG7 89 E4
Theydon Bois CM16 68 A1
Abridge Way IG11 153 B3
Acacia Ave RM12 135 F2
Acacia Ct EN9 66 A5
Acacia Dr Maldon CM9 36 F1
Southend-on-S SS1 168 A8
Upminster RM14 156 A8
Acacia Gdns RM14 137 F4
Acacia Rd Basildon SS13 143 E8
Greenhithe DA9 176 E1
Acacias Ct EN11 21 A6
Accrington Ho 10 RM3 114 D5
Acer Ave RM13 155 D2
Aconbury Rd RM9 153 B4
Acorn Cl E4 109 B5
Acorn Ct IG2 133 E6
Acorn Ctr The IG6 112 B4
Acorn Mews CM18 24 A6
Acorn Pl SS16 141 B5
Acorn Trad Est RM20 177 D8
Acorns The Chigwell IG7 111 E6
Hockley SS5 124 E7
Acre Rd RM10 154 B5
Acres Ave CM5 48 F5
Acres End CM1 31 E4
Acres The SS17 160 F3
Ada Cole Meml Stables Horse Sanctuary CM19 22 E4
Adalia Cres SS9 146 B3
Adalia Way SS9 146 B2
Adam Bsns Ctr SS14 120 F1
Adam Way SS11 121 E8
Adam's Elm Ho SS9 146 E2
Adams Glade SS4 125 D6
Adams Ho CM20 10 D1
Adams Rd SS17 160 E1
Addison Gdns RM17 173 C2
Addison Rd Redbridge IG6 111 C2
Wanstead E11 132 A5
Adelaide Gdns
Dagenham RM6 134 E6
South Benfleet SS7 144 D1
Adelaide Rd Ilford IG1 133 B2
Adelaide Rd *continued*
Tilbury RM18 178 F6
Adeliza Cl IG11 152 C5
Adelphi Cres RM12 136 B2
Adelsburg Rd SS8 164 C4
Aden Rd IG1 133 C4
Adingtons CM20 10 F2
Admirals Cl E18 132 B7
Admirals Lodge RM1 135 F6
Admirals Wlk
Chelmsford CM1 31 F3
Greenhithe DA9 177 B2
Hoddesdon EN11 21 B4
Southend-on-S SS3 168 D5
Adomar Rd RM8 134 E1
Adstock Way RM17 172 F2
Advice Ave RM16 173 A4
Afflets Ct SS14 142 C8
Afton Dr RM15 172 B7
Agister Rd IG7 112 A5
Agnes Ave Ilford IG1 152 B8
Southend-on-S SS9 146 B2
Agnes Gdns RM8 153 D8
Agricultural/Domestic Mus CM9 38 E7
Aidan Cl RM8 153 E8
Ailsa Rd SS0 166 C8
Ainsley Ave RM7 135 C5
Ainsley Wood Prim Sch E4 109 B5
Ainslie Wood Cres E4 109 B5
Ainslie Wood Gdns E4 109 B5
Ainslie Wood Rd E4 109 B5
Aintree Cres IG6 111 C1
Aintree Gr RM14 136 F1
Airborne Cl SS9 146 E5
Airborne Ind Est SS9 146 E5
Aire Dr RM15 157 B1
Airey Neave Ct RM16 173 A4
Airlie Gdns IG1 133 B3
Airport Ret Pk SS2 147 E6
Airthrie Rd IG3 134 B2
Akenfield Cl 1 CM3 101 E7
Alamein Gdns DA2 176 D1
Alamein Rd
Burnham-on-C CM0 106 C4
Chelmsford CM1 31 F6
Swanscombe DA10 177 D1
Alan Cl SS9 146 E6
Alan Gdns RM7 135 A4
Alan Gr SS9 146 E6
Albany Ave SS0 147 E1
Albany Cl CM1 31 E5
Albany Ct Chingford E4 87 B3
Epping CM16 45 F1
Albany Rd Dagenham RM6 134 F5
Hornchurch RM12 136 A2
Pilgrims Hatch CM15 94 B3
Rayleigh SS6 124 A1
Tilbury RM18 179 A6
Wickford SS12 121 D6
Albany Sch The RM12 136 B2
Albany The IG8 109 F6
Albany View IG9 88 A1
Albemarle App IG1 133 B5
Albemarle Cl RM17 173 A4
Albemarle Gdns IG2 133 B5
Albert Ave E4 109 A6
Albert Cl Grays RM16 173 C3
Rayleigh SS6 123 F3
Rochford SS4 125 C6
Albert Cres E4 109 A6
Albert Dr SS15 141 C6
Albert Gdns CM17 24 D7
Albert Ho 5 E18 132 B8
Albert Mews Romford RM1 135 F5
Southend-on-S SS0 166 E8
Albert Rd Belvedere DA17 169 A1
Buckhurst Hill IG9 110 D8
Bulphan RM14 158 F8
Burnham-on-C CM0 106 C5
Dagenham RM8 135 A3
Ilford IG1 133 C1
Rayleigh SS6 123 F3
Rochford SS4 125 C7
Romford RM1 135 F5
South Benfleet SS7 144 B6
South Woodham F CM3 101 D7
Southend-on-S, Bournes Green SS1 149 A1
Southend-on-S, Clifftown SS1 167 B7
Swanscombe DA10 177 F1
4 Wanstead E18 132 B8
Albert St CM14 116 C5
Albert Terr IG9 110 E8
Albion Cl RM7 135 D5
Albion Ct Billericay CM12 97 A1
5 Chelmsford CM2 32 B1
Albion Hill IG10 88 D4
Albion Pk IG10 88 D4
Albion Rd
Dagenham RM10 154 A7
Gravesend DA12 179 D1
South Benfleet SS7 144 D4
Southend-on-S SS0 147 E1
Albion Terr
Gravesend DA12 179 D1
Sewardstone E4 87 B5
Albra Mead CM2 33 B4
Albright Ind Est RM13 169 F8
Albury SS2 148 E2
Albury Mews E12 132 C2
Albyns SS16 141 C4
Albyns Cl RM13 155 A5
Albyns La
Stapleford Tawney RM4 91 D7
Stapleford Tawney RM4 91 E6
Alcester Ho 14 RM3 114 D5
Alcotes SS14 142 F5
Aldborough Ct
Chingford E4 109 B7
Ilford IG2 133 F6
Aldborough Rd
Dagenham RM10 154 C6
Ilford IG2 133 F8
Upminster RM14 137 A2
Aldborough Rd N IG2 133 F6
Aldborough Rd S IG3 133 E4
Aldeburgh Pl IG8 110 A6
Aldeburgh Way CM1 32 D5
Alder Ave RM14 155 F8
Alder Cl Basildon SS15 119 D1
Hoddesdon EN11 21 B8
Alder Dr Chelmsford CM2 54 B6
South Ockendon RM15 157 C1
Alderbury Lea CM3 56 F1
Aldergrove Wlk RM12 155 C6
Alderleys SS7 145 A6
Alderman Ave IG11 153 A2
Alderman Wlk SS17 160 E5
Alderman's Hill SS5 124 C5
Alderney Gdns SS11 99 C2
Alders Ave IG8 109 E4
Alders Cl E11 132 B2
Alders Wlk CM21 1 E2
Aldersbrook House Coll of Railway Tech E12 133 A1
Aldersbrook La E12 132 F1
Aldersbrook Prim Sch E12 132 C2
Aldersbrook Rd E12 132 C2
Aldersey Gdns IG11 152 D6
Aldersgrove EN9 65 E5
Alderton Cl Loughton IG10 89 A5
Pilgrims Hatch CM15 94 B4
Alderton Cty Jun & Inf Schs The IG10 89 A4
Alderton Hall La IG10 89 A5
Alderton Hill IG10 88 F4
Alderton Mews IG10 89 A5
Alderton Rd RM16 174 E7
Alderton Rise IG10 89 A5
Alderton Way IG10 88 F4
Alderwood Cl RM4 90 B6
Alderwood Dr RM4 90 B6
Alderwood Way SS7 145 C3
Aldham Dr RM15 172 C8
Aldham Gdns SS6 122 F3
Aldham Hall 1 E11 132 A5
Aldingham Ct RM12 155 B7
Aldingham Gdns RM12 155 A7
Aldington Cl RM8 134 C3
Aldria Rd SS17 160 E5
Aldriche Way E4 109 C4
Aldridge Ave EN3 65 A1
Aldridge Cl CM2 33 A4
Aldrin Cl SS17 160 E2
Aldrin Way SS9 147 A6
Aldwych Ave IG6 133 C7
Aldwych Cl RM12 136 B2
Alexander Ct
1 Chelmsford CM1 32 E7
Romford RM7 135 D3
Alexander La CM15 95 B4
Alexander Mews CM2 55 D2
Alexander Rd
Basildon SS16 141 B4
Greenhithe DA9 177 C2
Alexandra Cl RM16 174 C4
Alexandra Ct
Southend-on-S, Clifftown SS1 166 F7
Southend-on-S, Porters Town SS2 147 F1
Alexandra Rd
Brentwood CM14 116 C7
Burnham-on-C CM0 106 C5
Dagenham RM6 134 E5
Great Wakering SS3 150 A3
Rainham RM13 154 F4
Rayleigh SS6 123 F3
Rochford SS4 125 C7
Romford RM1 135 F5
South Benfleet SS7 144 D2
Southend-on-S, Clifftown SS1 166 F7
Southend-on-S, Leigh Cliffs SS9 165 E8
Tilbury RM18 178 F5
Wallend E6 152 A2
Wanstead E18 132 B8
Alexandra St SS1 167 A7
Alexandra Way RM18 175 B3
Alexandria Dr SS6 123 A4
Alf Lowne Ct RM16 174 A3
Alfred Gdns SS11 99 D1
Alfred Prior Ho 6 E12 152 A8
Alfred Rd Aveley RM15 171 C5
Brentwood CM14 116 D8
Buckhurst Hill IG9 110 D8
Alfred St RM17 178 C8
Alfred's Gdns IG11 152 E3
Alfred's Way (East Ham & Barking By-Pass) IG11 152 D3
Alfred's Way Ind Est IG11 153 A4
Alfreda Ave SS5 101 D3
Algars Way CM3 101 D8
Algers Cl IG10 88 D4
Algers Rd IG10 88 E4
Alghers Mead IG10 88 D4
Alibon Gdns RM10 154 A7
Alicia Ave SS11 122 A7
Alicia Cl SS11 122 A7
Alicia Way SS11 122 A7
Alicia Wlk SS11 122 A8
Alkerden La DA10 177 C1
All Saints CE Prim Sch
Maldon CM9 36 E2
Maldon CM9 36 F3
All Saints Cl
Chelmsford CM1 32 E4
Chigwell IG7 112 A7
Doddinghurst CM15 72 B3
Swanscombe DA10 177 F2
All Saints RC Sch RM8 135 A3
Allandale SS7 145 A7
Allandale Rd RM11 135 F4
Allen Rd RM13 155 C2
Allenby Cres RM17 173 C1
Allenby Dr RM11 136 F3
Allens Cl CM3 20 F1
Allens Rd CM11 98 C5
Allensway SS17 160 F3
Allerton Cl SS4 125 C6
Alley Dock SS9 165 D8
Alleyn Court Prep Sch SS3 149 A3
Alleyn Pl SS0 147 C1
Alleyndale Rd RM8 134 C2
Allison Cl EN9 66 A7
Allistonway SS17 160 F3
Allmains Cl EN9 44 B6
Allnutts Rd CM16 68 A6
Alloa Rd IG3 134 A2
Allysum Wlk CM12 96 F5
Alma Ave Chingford E4 109 C3
Hornchurch RM12 136 E1
Alma Cl South Benfleet SS7 146 A2
Wickford SS12 121 A6
Alma Dr CM1 32 A2
Alma Rd
South Benfleet SS7 146 A2
Swanscombe DA10 177 F2
Almere SS7 144 D4
Almond Ave SS12 121 C7
Almond Cl RM16 174 A3
Almond Wlk SS8 163 F4
Almonds Ave IG9 110 A8
Almshouses
Brentwood CM14 115 E8
Ingatestone CM4 74 B3
Almshouses The IG11 152 C6
Almshouses (Whitakers Charity) IG10 88 F8
Alnwick Cl SS16 140 F5
Alnwick Ct 6 DA2 176 B1
Alonso Ct 4 DA17 169 A1
Alp Ct SS3 150 A3
Alpha Cl SS13 143 F6
Alpha Rd Basildon SS13 143 F6
Brentwood CM13 95 D3
Burnham-on-C CM0 106 C5
Chingford E4 109 B7
Alracks SS15 141 E6
Alresford Gn SS12 121 E6
Altar Pl SS15 141 C7
Altham Gr CM20 10 F3
Althorne Cl SS13 121 B1
Althorne Sta CM3 104 F8
Althorne Way
Canewdon SS4 104 E2
Dagenham RM10 135 A2
Althorpe Cl SS5 124 D6
Alton Gdns SS2 147 E5
Aluric Cl RM16 174 B2
Alverstoke Rd RM3 114 E3
Alverstone Rd E12 152 A8
Alwen Gr RM15 172 B8
Alwyne Ave CM15 95 A3
Alyssum Cl CM1 33 A6
Amanda Cl IG7 111 D4
Amberden SS15 141 D5
Amberley Rd IG9 88 C1
Amberley Way RM7 135 B7
Amberry Ct CM20 10 D1
Ambleside Epping CM16 68 A8
Wickford SS11 122 B7
Ambleside Ave RM12 155 B7
Ambleside Dr SS1 167 D8
Ambleside Gdns
Hullbridge SS5 101 D2
Redbridge IG4 132 E6
Ambleside Wlk SS8 163 F5
Ambrook Rd DA17 169 A3
Ameland Rd SS8 164 A6
Amelia Blackwell Ho SS8 163 E3
America St CM9 37 A2
Amersham Ave SS16 140 F5
Amersham Cl RM3 114 F4
Amersham Dr RM3 114 F4
Amersham Rd RM3 114 F4
Amersham Wlk RM3 114 F4
Amery Gdns RM2 136 D8
Ames Rd DA10 177 E1
Amesbury EN9 66 A7
Amesbury Cl CM16 67 F8
Amesbury Dr E4 87 B3
Amesbury Rd
Dagenham RM9 153 D5
Epping CM16 67 F8
Amid Rd SS8 164 C5
Amidas Gdns RM8 153 B8
Amoss Rd CM2 54 F8
Ampers End SS14 142 D6
Ampthill Ho 2 RM3 114 D5
Amwell Ct Hoddesdon EN11 21 A7
Waltham Abbey EN9 65 E6
Amwell La SG12 8 B5
Amwell St EN11 21 A7
Amwell View Sch SG12 8 B4
Anchor Bvd DA2 176 D3
Anchor Dr RM13 155 B2
Anchor Ho IG3 134 A1
Anchor La
Abbess Roding CM5 14 C4
Canewdon SS4 104 E1
Heybridge CM9 37 A5
Anchor Lane Cotts SS4 104 E1
Anchor Par SS4 104 E1
Anchor Reach CM3 101 E5
Anchor St CM2 32 B1
Anchorage The
Burnham-on-C CM0 106 C3
Canvey Island SS8 164 B1
Great Wakering SS3 150 B4
Anders Fall SS9 147 A6
Anderson Ave CM1 31 F5
Anderson Ho IG11 152 D3
Anderson Rd IG8 132 D8
Anderson Way DA17 169 C4
Andersons SS17 160 F3
Andrea Ave RM16 173 A4
Andrew Cl Redbridge IG6 111 D3
Stanford-le-H SS17 160 D4
Andrews Cl IG9 110 C8
Andrews Pl CM1 31 F3
Andromeda Ct RM3 114 C4
Andy Hill Ho CM14 116 B6
Andyk Rd SS8 164 E7
Anerley Rd SS0 166 D8
Angel Cl SS16 142 D3
Angel Terr SS3 149 D2
Angel Way RM1 135 E6
Angle Gn RM8 134 C3
Angle Rd RM20 177 D8
Anglesea Ctr 3 DA11 179 B1
Anglesea Pl 2 DA11 179 B1
Anglesey Dr RM13 155 A1
Anglesey Gdns SS12 121 F5
Anglia Ctr The RM13 169 E8
Anglia Poly Univ
Chelmsford CM1 32 B4
Shenfield CM15 94 D1
Anglia Univ CM1 32 B2
Anglian Ind Est IG11 153 A1
Angmering Ho 1 RM3 114 D5
Ann Boleyn Dr SS4 147 F7
Annabell Ave RM16 174 D2
Annalee Gdns RM15 172 B8
Annalee Rd RM15 172 B8
Annan Way RM1 113 E2
Anne Boleyn Mans 4 SS13 143 B
Anne Nastri Ct RM2 136 B
Anne Way IG6 111 C
Annie Taylor Ho 1 E12 152 A
Anson Chase SS3 168 E
Anson Cl Romford RM7 113 B
South Woodham F CM3 101 F
Anstead Dr RM13 155 A
Anstey Cl SS9 146 D
Antelope Ave RM16 173 A
Anthony Cl CM11 119 D
Anthony Dr SS17 160 E
Antlers SS8 163 F
Antlers Hill E4 87 B
Anton Rd RM15 157 E
Antony Cl SS8 164 B
Antrim Rd SS3 168 D
Anvil Way Billericay CM12 97 B
Chelmsford CM1 32 E
Anworth Cl IG8 110 B
Apeldoorn SS7 144 B
Apex Ct SS5 124 E
Apollo Cl RM12 136 B
Apple Ct CM1 31 F
Apple Gate CM14 93 F
Apple Tree Cl CM15 72 D
Apple Tree Cres CM15 72 C
Apple Tree Way SS11 121 F
Apple Way CM2 54 D
Appleby Cl E4 109 C
Appleby Dr Basildon SS16 140 F
Romford RM3 114 C
Appleby Gn RM3 114 C
Appledene Cl SS6 123 D
Appledore SS3 149 C
Appledore Cl RM3 114 C
Appleford Ct 8 SS13 143 C
Applegarth Dr IG2 133 F
Applerow SS9 146
Appleton Cl CM19 23 C
Appleton Rd Loughton IG10 89 E
South Benfleet SS7 144 E
Appleton Sch The SS7 144
Appleton Way RM11 136
Appletree Cl SS2 148
Appleyard Ave SS5 124
Approach Rd
Basildon CM11 120 D
Canvey Island SS8 164
Approach The
Rayleigh SS6 123
Upminster RM14 137
April Pl CM21 1
Apton Hall Rd SS4 126
Arabia Cl E4 87
Araglen Ave RM15 172
Aragon Cl Loughton IG10 88
Romford RM5 113
Southend-on-S SS2 147
Aragon Ct IG6 111
Aragon Dr IG6 111
Arandora Cres RM6 134
Arbor Rd E4 109
Arbour Cl CM14 116
Arbour La CM1 32
Arbour Way RM12 155
Arbutus Cl CM2 54

Browns Cotts RM16 172 E5
Broxbourne Ave E18 132 B7
Broxbourne Rd E7 132 A1
Broxbourne Sta EN10 21 A3
Broxburn Dr RM15 172 B6
Broxburn Par RM15 172 B6
Broxhill Rd
Havering-atte-B RM4 114 B7
Romford RM4 113 F7
Broxted Dr SS12 121 E6
Broxted End 5 SS12 121 E6
Broxted Mews CM13 95 C3
Bruce Ave RM12 136 D2
Bruce Gr Chelmsford CM2 54 A7
Wickford SS11 122 A7
Bruce Rd CM1 31 B1
Bruces Wharf Rd RM17 178 A8
Bruges Rd SS8 164 C3
Brundish SS13 143 A5
Brunel Cl RM18 179 B5
Brunel Rd Chigwell IG8 110 F5
South Benfleet SS7 144 D7
Southend-on-S SS9 146 C7
Brunel Way CM3 101 C7
Brunswick Ave RM14 137 E4
Brunswick Ct
Hoddesdon EN11 21 A5
Upminster RM14 137 E4
Brunswick Gdns IG6 111 C3
Brunswick Lodge 6 E4 109 C8
Brunswick Pl SS6 123 B5
Brunswick Rd
Holdbrook EN3 65 A1
Southend-on-S SS1 167 D7
Brunswick Wlk DA12 179 D1
Brunwins Cl SS11 121 F8
Brushwood Lodge DA17 169 A2
Brussum Rd SS8 164 D2
Bruton Ave SS0 147 A5
Bryanston Rd RM18 179 C5
Bryant Ave Romford RM3 114 D1
Southend-on-S SS1 167 E6
Bryant Row RM3 114 C8
Bryant's La CM9 57 D7
Bryce Rd RM8 153 C8
Bryn Farm Cl SS14 142 C8
Bryony Cl IG10 89 B5
Buchanan Cl RM15 171 C5
Buchanan Gdns SS12 121 E5
Buchanan Way CM3 82 B5
Buckbean Path RM3 114 C3
Buckeridge Way CM0 42 B3
Buckerills SS13 143 A6
Buckhatch La CM3 78 D3
Buckhurst Hill Cty Prim Sch IG9 110 E8
Buckhurst Hill Ho IG9 110 B8
Buckhurst Hill Sta IG9 110 D8
Buckhurst Way IG9 110 D7
Buckingham Cl RM11 136 D6
Buckingham Ct 2 CM2 32 F4
Buckingham Hill Rd
Linford SS17, RM16 174 F5
Stanford-le-H SS17 175 A7
Buckingham Rd
Basildon SS15 141 E8
Hockley SS5 124 D6
Ilford IG1 133 D2
Wanstead E11 132 C6
Woodford E18 109 F2
Buckinghamshire Sq SS11 122 A5
Buckland SS3 149 C1
Buckland Gate CM3 101 C6
Bucklebury Heath CM3 101 D6
Bucklers Ct CM14 116 C5
Buckles La RM15 172 D8
Buckley Cl SS17 160 F5
Buckleys CM2 54 F7
Buckleys Yd RM13 170 A8
Bucknells Mead CM1 52 A4
Buckrell Rd E4 109 D8
Buckwins Sq SS13 121 D1
Buckwyns Chase CM12 96 F6
Buckwyns Ct CM12 96 F4
Budna Rd SS8 163 F5
Budoch Ct IG3 134 A2
Budoch Dr IG3 134 A2
Buglers Rise CM1 53 B8
Bulbecks Wlk CM3 101 D5
Bulimers Way CM1 52 F8
Bull Cl Basildon SS16 142 E5
Grays RM16 172 F4
Bull La Dagenham RM10 135 B1
Hockley SS5 124 C6
Maldon CM9 37 A3
Rayleigh SS6 123 E2
Bullbanks Rd DA17 169 C2
Bullen Ct IG6 111 E4
Bullen Wlk CM2 54 C3
Buller Rd Barking IG11 152 E5
Basildon SS15 141 B7
North Fambridge CM3 81 A1
Bullfields CM21 1 E3
Bullivant Cl DA9 177 A2
Bulls Lodge Cotts CM3 20 B1
Bullwood App SS5 124 B5
Bullwood Hall La SS5 124 A4
Bullwood Rd SS5 124 D5
Bulmers Wlk RM13 155 C3
Bulow Ave SS8 164 B3
Bulphan By-Pass RM14 140 A1
Bulphan Cl SS12 121 E6
Bulphan Cty Prim Sch RM14 158 F8
Bulwark Rd SS3 168 E8
Bumbles Green La EN9 44 B6
Bumfords La CM3, CM9 35 A7
Bunces La IG8 109 F3
Bundick's Hill CM1 31 F3
Bungalows The
Abbess Roding CM5 14 E3
Grays RM20 177 A8
Bunters Ave SS3 168 C6
Bunting Cl CM2 54 B5
Bunting La CM11 97 C1
Buntingbridge Rd IG2 133 D6
Burch Rd DA11 178 F1
Burches SS14 119 E1
Burches Mead SS7 145 A7
Burches Rd SS7 144 F8
Burchett Way RM6 134 F5
Burchwall Cl RM5 113 C3
Burden Way E11 132 B2
Burdett Ave SS0 166 E8
Burdett Rd SS1 167 C7
Burdetts Rd RM9 153 F4
Bure RM18 175 C3
Buren Ave SS8 164 E3
Burfield Cl SS9 146 F6
Burfield Rd SS9 146 F6
Burford Cl Dagenham RM8 134 C1
Ilford IG6 133 C7
Burford Gdns EN11 21 B7
Burford Mews 9 EN11 21 A7
Burford Pl 11 EN11 21 A7
Burges Cl
Hornchurch RM11 136 F5
Southend-on-S SS1 168 C6
Burges Rd
Southend-on-S SS1 168 B6
Wallend E6 152 A5
Burges Terr SS1 167 F6
Burgess Ave SS17 160 E1
Burgess Ct
Brentwood CM15 94 C1
Wallend E12 152 A5
Burgess Field CM2 32 F4
Burghley Rd RM16 172 C3
Burghstead Cl CM12 97 A1
Burgoyne Hatch CM20 11 A1
Burgundy Ct CM2 32 C2
Burgundy Gdns 6 SS13 143 B8
Burham Bsns Pk CM0 106 A6
Burham-on-Crouch Sta CM0 106 B6
Burland Rd
Brentwood CM15 94 D1
Romford RM5 113 C4
Burleigh Cl CM12 97 B5
Burleigh Ct SS1 168 B8
Burleigh Mans SS0 166 C8
Burleigh Sq SS1 168 B8
Burlescoombe Cl SS1 168 A8
Burlescoombe Leas SS1 149 B1
Burlescoombe Rd SS1 149 A1
Burley Cl E4 109 A5
Burley Hill CM17 24 D7
Burlington Ave RM7 135 B5
Burlington Ct SS13 143 B8
Burlington Gdns
Dagenham RM6 134 E4
Hullbridge SS5 123 F8
South Benfleet SS7 145 F3
Burlington Pl IG8 110 A7
Burnaby Rd
Gravesend DA11 178 E1
Southend-on-S SS1 167 C7
Burne Ave SS12 121 A6
Burnell Wlk CM13 116 C4
Burnels Ave E6 152 A2
Burnett Pk CM19 23 B3
Burnett Rd DA8 170 D1
Burney Dr IG10 89 C6
Burnham Ave CM3 81 A5
Burnham Cres E11 132 C7
Burnham Rd Althorne CM3 83 B1
Battlesbridge SS11 100 E3
Chelmsford CM1 32 D5
Dagenham RM9 153 B4
Hullbridge SS5 101 E2
Latchingdon CM3 82 D5
Mundon CM9 81 C8
Romford RM7 135 D8
South Woodham F CM3 79 D1
Southend-on-S SS9 146 C1
Southminster CM0 84 C2
Woodham Mortimer CM9, CM3 57 E5
Burnham-on-Crouch Cty Prim Sch CM0 106 C5
Burnham-on-Crouch District Mus CM0 106 B4
Burnley Rd RM20 177 A6
Burns Ave Basildon SS13 143 B5
Dagenham RM6 134 C4
Burns Cl CM9 37 A1
Burns Cres CM2 54 C8
Burns Pl RM18 179 B6
Burns Way CM13 95 D3
Burnside
Canvey Island SS8 164 A5
Sawbridgeworth CM21 1 D2
Burnside Ave E4 109 A4
Burnside Cres CM1 32 B7
Burnside Ind Est IG6 112 B5
Burnside Rd RM8 134 C3
Burnside Terr CM17 11 F3
Burnt Ho IG7 89 F1
Burnt Mill CM20 10 C3
Burnt Mill Comp Sch CM20 10 F2
Burnt Mills Rd SS13 121 C1
Burnt Oak Lodge SS7 146 A2
Burnthouse La
Ingatestone CM4 73 F1
Burnthouse La *continued*
Mountnessing CM4, CM13 96 A8
Burntmill Cl CM20 10 C3
Burntmill Cnr CM20 10 D4
Burntmill La CM20 10 D3
Burntwood CM14 116 C7
Burntwood Ave RM11 136 E5
Burntwood Cl
Billericay CM12 96 F2
West Horndon CM13 139 D5
Burnway RM11 136 E4
Burr Cl SS16 140 E5
Burr Hill Chase SS2 147 E3
Burr's Way SS17 161 B4
Burrow Cl IG7 111 F5
Burrow Gn IG7 111 F5
Burrow Rd IG7 112 A5
Burrows Way SS6 123 C1
Burrswood Pl CM9 37 E3
Burses Way CM13 95 B2
Burslem Ave IG6 112 A4
Burstead Dr CM11 119 D7
Burton Cl SS17 160 F5
Burton Pl CM2 32 F4
Burton Rd Loughton IG10 89 C5
Wanstead E18 132 B8
Burtons Mill CM21 1 F3
Burwell Ave SS8 163 F5
Burwood Ct CM2 32 C1
Burwood Gdns RM13 154 F2
Bury Farm Cotts RM14 138 E2
Bury Farm La CM11 120 D3
Bury La Epping CM16 45 D2
Great Waltham CM3 18 D8
Bury Rd Chingford E4 87 E4
Dagenham RM10 154 C7
Epping CM16 67 E8
Harlow CM17 11 D4
Bush Cl IG2 133 D6
Bush Elms Rd RM11 136 A4
Bush Fair CM18 23 F6
Bush Hall Rd CM12 97 C5
Bush Ho CM18 23 F6
Bush Rd Wanstead E11 132 A4
Woodford IG9 110 D6
Bushey Cl Chingford E4 109 C7
South Woodham F CM3 101 E7
Bushey Croft CM18 23 E7
Bushfields IG10 89 A4
Bushgrove Rd RM8 134 D1
Bushway RM8 134 D1
Bushwood E11 132 A3
Bushy Lea CM5 49 A2
Bushy Mead SS15 141 B8
Business Ctr The RM3 114 D3
Bute Rd IG6 133 B6
Butler Ct RM8 135 A2
Butler Ho RM17 178 B8
Butler Rd RM8 153 B8
Butler Wlk RM17 173 D2
Butlers Cl CM1 19 B2
Butlers Dr E4 65 C1
Butlers Gr SS16 141 B3
Butneys SS14 142 B7
Butt La CM9 37 A3
Butt's Green Rd CM2 55 F3
Butterbur Chase CM3 101 C6
Buttercross La CM16 46 A1
Buttercup Cl
Billericay CM12 97 A4
Romford RM3 114 D2
Buttercup Way CM0 84 C3
Butterfield Rd CM3 33 E8
Butteridges Cl RM9 153 F4
Buttersweet Rise CM21 1 E1
Butterworth Gdns IG8 110 A5
Butterys SS1 167 E8
Buttfield Cl RM10 154 B6
Button Rd RM17 172 F2
Button's Hill CM3 83 B4
Butts Green Rd RM11 136 D5
Butts La Danbury CM3 56 F7
Stanford-le-H SS17 175 C8
Butts Paddock SS4 104 D2
Butts Rd
Great Wakering SS3 150 C1
Stanford-le-H SS17 160 C1
Butts Way CM2 53 E3
Buttsbury CM4 74 E1
Buttsbury Inf Sch The CM12 97 B5
Buttsbury Jun Sch The CM12 97 B5
Buttsbury Rd Ilford IG1 152 C7
Ilford IG1 152 D7
Buttsbury Terr CM4 75 E2
Buxton Ave SS9 146 A3
Buxton Cl
Southend-on-S SS9 146 A3
Woodford IG8 110 D4
Buxton Link SS15 140 E6
Buxton Lodge E11 132 B2
Buxton Rd Chingford E4 87 D2
Grays RM16 173 E4
Ilford IG2 133 E5
Theydon Bois CM16 67 E3
Waltham Abbey EN9 66 A6
Buxton Sq SS9 146 A3
Buyl Ave SS8 164 B5
By-Pass Rd SS17 160 A2
Byfield SS9 146 F7
Byfield Ct CM13 139 C5
Byfletts SS16 142 F4
Byford Rd SS6 123 E3
Bynghams CM19 22 F6
Byrd Ct SS15 141 C8
Byrd Mead CM15 72 A6
Byrd Way SS17 160 C3
Byrne Dr SS2 147 E5
Byron Ave
Southend-on-S SS2 148 B2
Woodford E18 109 F1
Byron Cl SS8 164 C4
Byron Ct Basildon SS15 141 B6
11 Wanstead E11 132 A7
Woodford E18 110 B2
Byron Gdns RM18 179 C6
Byron Mans RM14 137 C1
Byron Rd Brentwood CM13 95 D2
Chelmsford CM2 32 D2
Dartford DA1 176 B3
Byron Way RM3 114 C2
Byron Wks SS11 121 F7
Bysouth Cl IG5 111 B2
Bywater Rd CM3 101 C6

C

Cabborns Cres SS17 175 D8
Cabinet Way SS9 146 C6
Cables Cl DA8 169 C3
Cadiz Ct RM10 154 D5
Cadiz Rd RM10 154 C6
Cadogan Ave CM13 139 D5
Cadogan Gdns E18 132 B8
Cadogan Terr SS13 143 C7
Caernarvon Cl
Hockley SS5 124 D6
Hornchurch RM11 137 A3
Caernarvon Dr IG5 111 A2
Cage End CM22 3 F5
Cage End Cl CM22 3 F5
Cage Field Cotts SS4 126 D4
Cagefield Rd SS4 126 E4
Caidge Row CM0 42 A2
Cairns Ave IG8 110 F4
Caister Dr SS13 143 B6
Caladonia La 9 SS12 121 E5
Calbourne Ave RM12 155 B7
Calcott Cl CM14 94 B1
Calcutta Rd RM18 178 F5
Caldbeck EN9 65 D5
Calder RM18 175 C2
Caldwell Rd SS17 160 B1
Caldy Rd DA17 169 B3
Caledon Rd E6 152 A5
Caledonia Ct IG11 153 C3
Caledonia La SS12 121 E5
Caledonian Cl 1 IG3 134 B3
Callan Gr RM15 172 B6
Callowood Croft CM3 58 D1
Calmore Cl RM12 155 C7
Calmpatch 9 CM0 106 C4
Calne Ave IG5 111 B2
Calshot Ave RM16 172 F4
Calshot Ct 23 DA2 176 B1
Calverley Cres RM10 135 A2
Calvert Cl DA17 169 B2
Calvert Dr SS13 121 C1
Calverton Rd E6 152 A4
Cam Gn RM15 172 B7
Cambell Jun Sch RM9 153 D5
Cambeys Rd RM10 154 C7
Camborne Ave RM3 114 E3
Camborne Cl CM1 32 E5
Camborne Way RM3 114 E3
Cambria Cl SS8 163 C3
Cambrian Ave IG2 133 E6
Cambridge Ave RM2 136 C8
Cambridge Cl
Basildon SS16 140 F5
Stock CM4 75 D2
Cambridge Ct SS1 166 F7
Cambridge Gdns
Grays RM16 174 B2
Rochford SS4 125 C5
Cambridge Park Rd E11 132 A4
Cambridge Pk E11 132 A5
Cambridge Rd
Barking IG11 152 C5
Canvey Island SS8 163 F3
3 Chingford E4 87 D1
Harlow CM20 11 C6
Ilford IG3 133 E3
Sawbridgeworth CM21 1 E4
Southend-on-S SS1 166 F7
Camden Cl RM16 174 B2
Camden Ct 9 DA17 169 A1
Camden Rd Grays RM16 172 F3
Wanstead E11 132 B5
Camelford Ho 1 RM3 114 E6
Camelia Ct IG8 109 E4
Camellia Cl
2 Chelmsford CM1 32 F6
Romford RM3 114 E2
Camelot Cl CM1 31 F5
Camelot Gdns SS13 143 C8
Cameron Cl
Brentwood CM14 116 D6
Ingatestone CM4 74 B3
Southend-on-S SS9 146 C2
Stanford-le-H SS17 160 E6
Cameron Pl SS12 121 E5
Cameron Rd IG3 133 E3
Camms Terr RM10 154 C7
Camomile Dr SS11 121 E8
Camomile Rd RM7 135 E2
Campbell Ave IG6 133 C7
Campbell Cl
Chelmsford CM2 54 A7
Harlow CM17 24 B7
Romford RM1 113 E4
3 Wickford SS12 121 D5
Campden Cres RM8 153 C8
Camper Rd SS1 167 D6
Camperdown Rd SS8 164 C5
Campfield Rd SS3 168 E6
Campion Cl RM7 135 D2
Campion Ct RM17 178 D8
Campion Sch The RM11 136 F7
Campions Harlow CM17 11 F5
Loughton IG10 67 A1
Campions The SS1 168 C8
Cample La RM15 172 A6
Campsey Gdns RM9 153 B5
Campsey Rd RM9 153 B5
Can Bridge Way CM2 32 C1
Canal Basin DA12 179 D1
Canal Rd DA12 179 D1
Canal Road Ind Pk DA12 179 D1
Canberra Cl
Chelmsford CM1 31 E5
Dagenham RM10 154 D5
Hornchurch RM12 155 C8
Canberra Cres RM10 154 D5
Canberra Sq RM18 179 A5
Cander Way RM15 172 B6
Candlemakers The SS2 148 A5
Candover Rd RM12 136 B3
Candy Terr 12 SS1 167 C7
Candytuft Rd CM1 32 F6
Cane Hill RM3 114 D1
Caneland Ct EN9 65 F5
Canes La CM17 24 E1
Canewdon Cl SS11 99 D2
Canewdon Gdns SS11 99 D2
Canewdon Hall Cl SS4 104 D2
Canewdon Prim Sch SS4 104 E1
Canewdon Rd
Rochford SS4 125 D8
Southend-on-S SS0 166 D8
Canewdon View Rd SS4 125 D6
Canfield Rd High Roding CM6 5 E8
Rainham RM13 154 F4
Woodford IG8 110 E3
Canford Ave SS12 120 F8
Canford Cl CM2 54 E7
Canney Rd CM0 61 D4
Cannington Rd RM9 153 C6
Cannon Ct SS13 121 A2
Cannon Leys CM2 54 D3
Cannon Mews EN9 65 B6
Cannons La Fyfield CM5 27 E1
Hatfield Broad Oak CM22 3 F5
Cannons Mead CM15 72 A6
Cannons Villas CM22 3 F5
Canon Ave RM6 134 C6
Canon Cl SS17 160 F2
Canon Palmer RC High Sch IG3 133 E3
Canons Brook CM19 23 B8
Canons Cl CM3 56 E1
Canons Gate CM20 10 A2
Canonsleigh Cres SS9 146 E1
Canonsleigh Rd RM9 153 B5
Canterbury Ave
Redbridge IG1 132 E4
Southend-on-S SS2 148 E3
Upminster RM14 137 F2
Canterbury Cl
8 Basildon SS14 142 F8
Chigwell IG7 111 F7
Rayleigh SS6 123 C5
Canterbury Ct CM15 93 F4
Canterbury Ho 2 IG11 153 A5
Canterbury Par RM15 157 C2
Canterbury Pl RM17 173 D1
Canterbury Way
Chelmsford CM1 31 E4
Dartford DA2 176 D5
Great Warley CM13 116 C4
Canters The SS7 145 B5
Cantley Gdns IG2 133 C5
Canuden Rd CM1 31 E2
Canute Cl SS4 104 E2
Canvey Cty Jun & Inf Schs SS8 163 F3
Canvey Rd Basildon SS13 143 F6
Canvey Island SS8 163 D5
Southend-on-S SS9 146 B1
Canvey Way SS7 144 A3
Canvey Wlk CM1 32 E6
Capadocia St SS1 167 E6
Cape Cl IG11 152 B5
Capel Cl Chelmsford CM1 32 B7
Stanford-le-H SS17 160 E2
Capel Gdns IG3 152 F8
Capel Terr SS1 167 A7
Capelston SS15 141 F6
Capital Pl CM19 23 A7
Capitol Ind Ctr SS11 122 A5
Capon Cl CM14 94 B1
Capons La CM3 57 A5
Capricorn Ctr
Basildon SS14 120 F1
Dagenham RM8 134 F4
Capstan Cl RM6 134 B5
Capstan Ct DA2 176 C3
Capstan Ctr RM18 178 D7
Caravan Site The RM15 171 D3
Caravel Cl RM16 172 F3
Carbis Cl E4 87 D1
Carbury Cl RM12 155 C6
Card's Rd CM2 55 C6
Cardigan Ave SS0 147 C3
Cardigan Gdns IG3 134 A2
Cardigan Ho 4 RM3 114 D5
Cardinal Dr IG6 111 C4
Cardinal Way RM13 155 D3
Carey Ho SS0 166 E8

H

Halcyon Way RM11 ....136 F3
Haldan Rd E4 ....109 C4
Haldon Cl **3** IG7 ....111 E5
Hale Cl E4 ....109 C7
Hale Cotts DA9 ....117 D2
Hale End RM3 ....114 B4
Hale End Rd E17 ....109 D2
Hale Ho M11 ....136 A5
Hale The E4 ....109 D3
Halesworth El RM3 .....114 E3
Halesworth Rd RM11 ...114 E4
Half Moon Cotts CM21 ..1 B1
Half Moon La CM16 .....67 F8
Halfhides EN9 ....65 D6
Halfway St RM19 ....171 A2
Halidon Rise M7 ....115 B4
Halifax Ho **El** RM3 .....115 B4
Hall Ave RM15 ....171 C5
Hall Bridge Rise CM9 ...37 C4
Hall Chase CM6 ....7 D8
Hall Cl Great Baddow CM2 ..54 C3
  Stanford-le-H SS17 ...160 E4
Hall Cres Aveley RM15 ..171 C4
  South Benfleet SS7 ...145 D3
Hall Est CM9 ....38 E7
Hall Farm Ct RM7 ......144 D1
Hall Farm Cl SS7 ......144 D1
Hall Green La CM13 ....95 D2
Hall La Brentwood CM15 .95 A6
  Chelmsford CM2 ....55 C6
  Chingford E4 ....37 B4
  Inglestone CM4 ....74 C1
  Romford RM11 ....115 C1
  Shenfield CM15 ....94 F4
  Shenfield CM15 ....94 F6
  South Ockendon RM15 ..157 E4
  Upminster RM14 ....137 D5
  West Hanningfield CM2 .76 D6
Hall Mark Ind Est CM0 ..84 E4
Hall Park Ave SS0 .....166 B8
Hall Park Rd RM14 .....156 C7
Hall Rd Asheldham CM0 ..85 C7
  Aveley RM15 ....171 C4
  Hockley SS5 ....125 A2
  Ilford RM6 ....134 D5
  Maldon CM9 ....37 B4
  Rochford SS4 ....125 D1
  Romford RM2 ....136 B8
  Southminster CM0 .....84 E4
Hall St CM2 ....32 B1
Hall Terr Aveley RM15 ..171 D4
  Harold Wood RM3 ......115 A3
Hallam Cl CM15 ....72 B3
Hallam Cl CM2 ....96 F4
Hallet Rd SS3 ....164 E3
Halling Hill CM20 .....10 F2
Hallingbury Rd CM21 ....2 A4
Hallmores EN10 ....24 A1
Hallowell Down CM5 ....101 E6
Hallsford Bridge Ind Est CM5 ..71 C8

Halsham Cres SS13 ....157 F7
Halstead Cl **El** SS12 ...122 C5
Halstead Ho **El** RM3 ...114 D4
Halstead Rd E11 ....132 B6
Halstead Way CM11 .....95 C3
Halston Ct SS17 ....161 B4
Halston Pl CM9 ....38 B8
Halstow Way SS13 ......143 C5
Halt Dr SS17 ....175 B2
Halt Robin La DA17 ....169 B2
Halt Robin Rd DA17 ....169 B2
Halton Rd RM16 ....174 C3
Haltwhistle Rd CM8 ....101 C8
Halyard Reach CM3 ....101 E5
Hamberts Rd CM3 ....79 E1
Hamble La RM15 ....171 F8
Hamboro Gdns CM9 .....106 A6
Hamboro Gdns SS6 .....146 B1
Hambro Ave SS6 ....123 E4
Hambro Cl SS6 ....123 E4
Hambro Hill SS6 ......123 E4
Hambro Rd CM15 ....110 D8
Hamden Cres RM10 .....135 E3
Hamelin Ho RM3 ....114 D2
Hamerton Rd RM12 .....178 B2
Hameway E6 ....152 A1
Hamilton Ave
  Hoddesdon EN11 ......21 A8
  Ilford IG6 ....133 C6
  Romford RM11 ....113 D1
Hamilton Cl SS11 .....123 C4
Hamilton Cres CM14 ...106 C4
Hamilton Cl **El** CM0 ...2 A4
Hamilton Dr RM3 ......114 E1
Hamilton Gdns SS5 ....124 E7
Hamilton Mews SS6 ....123 F3
Hamilton Rd Ilford IG1 ..132 B8
  Romford RM2 ....136 A1
Hamlet Cl RM5 ....113 C2
Hamlet Court Mews SS0 ..147 E1
Hamlet Court Rd SS0 ...166 E8
Hamlet Ct CM14 ....145 C8
Hamlet Est DA8 ....169 D1
Hamlet Hill CM19 ......22 B4
Hamlet Rd Chelmsford CM2 ..32 B1
  Romford RM5 ....113 C2
  Southend-on-S SS1 ...166 F7
Hamley Cl SS7 ....144 B6
Hammarskjold Rd SS0 ..200 D2
Hammond Ct RM12 .....135 F3
Hammonds Rd RM8 .....134 C1
Hammonds La
  Billericay CM11 .....119 C7
  Great Warley CM11 ...116 B4

Hammonds Rd
  Hatfield Broad Oak CM22 ..4 A6
  Little Baddow CM3 ....33 E3
Hampden Cl CM16 ......47 A4
Hampden Cres CM14 ....116 C5
Hampden Gdns RM3 .....173 B1
Romford RM5 ....113 B3
Hampshire Gdns SS17 ..175 A4
Hampshire Rd M11 .....137 A7
Hampstead Gdns SS3 ...124 F7
Hampton Cl SS2 ....147 E4
Hampton Ct Hockley SS5 ..124 D6
  Southend-on-S,
  Chalkwell SS9 ....165 F8
  Southend-on-S,
  Leigh-on-S SS9 ......146 E1
Hampton Gdns
  Sawbridgeworth CM21 ..11 C7
  Southend-on-S SS2 ...147 E4
Hampton Mead IG10 ....89 B6
Hampton Rd Chingford E4 ..109 A5
  Great Baddow CM2 ....54 E6
  Ilford IG1 ....152 C8
Hamstel Rd Harlow CM20 ..10 C1
  Southend-on-S SS2 ...148 D2
Hamstel Road Schs SS2 ..148 D2
Hanbury Rd CM1 ....53 E8
Hand La CM21 ....1 C1
Handel Cres RM18 .....179 A7
Handel Rd SS8 ....164 D2
Handforth Rd **El** SS1 ...133 B1
Handley Gn SS15 ......141 C5
Handleys Chase SS15 ..119 F2
Handleys Ct SS15 .....119 F2
Handsworth Ave E4 ....109 D4
Handsworth Prim Sch E4 ..109 D4
Handtrough Way IG11 ..152 B3
Hanford Rd RM15 .....171 C5
Hanging Hill CM13 ....95 C2
Hanging Hill La CM13 ..117 B8
Hanlee Brook CM2 ....54 F5
Hannah Cl SS8 ....164 A6
Hannards Way IG6 ....112 B6
Hannett Rd SS8 ......164 B3
Hanningfield Cl SS4 ..123 A3
Hanover Cl SS14 .....142 E5
Hanover Ct
  Hoddesdon EN11 .....21 A7
  Rayleigh SS6 ....123 D3
  Waltham Abbey EN9 ..65 C6
Hanover Dr SS14 .....142 E6
Hanover Gdns IG6 ....111 C3
Hanover Mead CM17 ...22 B8
Hanson Cl IG10 ......89 C7
Hanover Mews SS6 ....146 B8
Hanson Dr IG10 ......89 C7
Hanson Gn IG10 ......89 C7
Harberts Rd CM19 ....23 B8
Harberts Way SS6 ....123 C5
Harbourer Cl IG6 ....112 B5
Harbourer Rd IG6 ....112 B5
Harcourt Ave SS2 ....147 F1
Harcourt Ho **6** E4 ....110 C4
Hard Cl IG8 ....110 C4
Hardcourt Mews RM2 ..135 F6
Hardie Rd
  Dagenham RM10 ......135 C1
  Stanford-le-H SS17 ..160 D2
Harding Rd RM16 .....174 A3
Harding's Elms Rd CM11 ..120 B4
Hardings La CM4 ....74 A7
Hardings Reach **El** CM0 ..106 C4
Hardley Cres RM11 ....136 D7
Hardwick Cl SS6 .....123 D1
Hardwick Ct
  Southend-on-S SS7 ...147 E3
  9 Wanstead E11 .....132 A2
Hardwicke St IG11 ....152 C4
Hardy SS3 ....168 C5
Hardy Cl **El** E11 ....132 A7
Hardy Gr DA1 ....176 A3
Hardys Way SS8 ......164 A6
Hare Hall La RM2 .....136 B7
Hare St SS13 ....143 A5
Hare Street Cty Jun & Inf
  Sch SS13 ....23 C8
Hare Street Springs CM19 ..23 B8
Hare Terr RM20 ....172 D1
Harebell Cl CM12 .....96 F4
Harebell Way RM3 ....114 D3
Harefield CM20 ....10 F1
Hares Chase CM12 ....96 F3
Haresfield Rd RM10 ...154 A6
Haresland Cl SS7 .....145 F6
Harewood Ave SS4 ....125 D5
Harewood Dr IG5 .....110 F1
Harewood Hill CM16 ..67 E4
Harewood Rd
  Chelmsford CM1 .....31 E1
  Haynes Hatch CM15 ..94 B3
Harford Cl E4 ....87 B2
Harford Rd E4 ....87 B2
Harfred Ave CM9 .....38 E7
Harkness Cl RM3 .....114 F5
Harlech Rd **El** SS13 ...143 B5
Harlequin Stps **16** SS11 ..167 C7
Harlesden Cl RM3 ....114 F4
Harlesden Rd RM3 ....114 F4
Harlesden Wlk RM3 ...114 F4
Harley Ct E11 ....132 A4
Harley St SS9 ....146 C1
Harlings Gn CM1 .....32 C3
Harlow Coll CM17 ....10 D1
Harlow Comm CM17 ...24 D6
Harlow Ct SS12 ......121 B1
Harlow Ho **El** IG11 ...152 B5
Harlow Mans **El** IG11 ..152 B5

Harlow Mill Sta CM20 ..11 C5
Harlow Rd Moreton CM5 ..26 C3
  Rainham RM13 ....154 F4
  Roydon CM19 ....9 C1
  Sawbridgeworth CM21 ..11 C8
  Sheering CM22, CM17 .12 B8
  Sheering, Matching Tye CM22 ..12 F3
Harlow Seedbed Ctr
  CM19 ....23 A7
Harlow Sports Ctr CM20 ..10 D2
Harlow Stad (Greyhounds)
  CM19 ....9 E1
Harlow Town Mus CM18 ..23 C7
Harlow Town Sta CM20 ..10 D3
Harlowbury Cty Prim Sch
  CM17 ....65 F5
Harlton Ct EN9 ....65 F5
Harman Ave IG8 ......109 F4
Harman Cl E4 ....109 D6
Harmer Rd DA10 ......177 F1
Harmer St DA12 ......179 C1
Harness Cl CM1 ......32 E7
Harold Cl CM19 ......22 F7
Harold Court Prim Sch
  RM3 ....115 A3
Harold Court Rd RM3 ..115 B3
Harold Cres EN9 .....65 E7
Harold Ct RM1 ....115 B3
Harold Gdns SS11 ....99 E1
Harold Hill Com Sch
  Romford RM3 ....114 C6
  Romford RM3 ....114 D6
Harold View RM3 .....114 F1
Harold Wood Hall RM3 ..114 C2
Harold Wood Hospl RM3 ..114 E2
Harold Wood Prim Sch
  RM11 ....137 A8
Harold Wood Sta RM3 ..114 F2
Harolds Rd CM19 .....22 F7
Haron Cl SS8 ....164 B2
Harpenden Rd E12 ....132 C2
Harper Way SS6 ......123 C3
Harpers La SS9 ......72 D2
Harpour Rd IG11 .....152 C6
Harrap Chase RM17 ...172 F1
Harridge Cl SS9 .....146 E3
Harridge Rd SS9 .....146 E3
Harrier Cl
  Hornchurch RM12 ....155 B6
  Southend-on-S SS3 ..149 E1
Harrier Way EN9 .....66 A7
Harriescourt EN9 ....66 A7
Harris Cl SS12 ......121 F5
Harris Ct SS5 ....124 E5
Harris Rd RM9 ....153 F7
Harrison Cl CM13 ....95 D4
Harrison Ct CM1 .....47 B5
Harrison Dr CM16 ....47 B5
Harrison Gdns SS5 ...101 D2
Harrison Rd RM10 ....154 B6
Harrisons Wharf RM17 ..171 A1
Harrods Ct CM11 .....97 D2
Harrogate Dr SS5 ....124 F8
Harrogate Rd SS5 ....124 F8
Harrold Rd RM8 ......153 B7
Harrow Cres SS11 ....114 B2
Harrow Dr RM11 .....136 C4
Harrow Gdns SS5 ....125 A5
Harrow Lodge RM11 ..136 C3
Harrow Lodge Campus
  RM11 ....136 B4
Harrow Rd Barking IG11 ..152 E4
  Basildon SS21 ......122 A2
  Canvey Island SS8 ...164 B5
  Ilford IG1 ....152 C8
  North Benfleet SS12 .121 F2
Harrow Way CM2 ......55 A6
Harston Dr EN3 ......65 F1
Hart Cl SS7 ....145 A6
Hart Cnr RM20 ......172 D1
Hart Cres IG7 ....111 F7
Hart Cl E4 ....152 A5
Hart Rd Harlow CM17 ..24 D8
  St Brentwood CM14 ...116 C8
Hart St Brentwood CM14 ..116 C8
  Chelmsford CM2 .....32 A1
Hartford Cl E4 ......109 B1
Hartford End SS13 ...143 A5
Hartington Pl SS1 ...167 B7
Hartington Rd SS1 ...167 B7
Hartland Cl SS9 .....146 D7
Hartland Rd Epping CM16 ..46 A1
  Hornchurch RM12 ....33 A4
Hartley Cl CM2 ......33 A4
Harts La IG11 ....152 A5
Hartshorn Gdns E6 ...152 A1
Hartswood Cl CM14 ...116 E6
Hartswood Hospl CM13 ..116 B4
Hartswood Rd CM13 ...116 C2
Hartwell Dr E4 ......109 C4
Harty Cl RM16 ......173 B5
Harvard Ave CM1 .....31 F4
Harvard Wlk RM11 ....155 A8
Harvest Cl IG10 .....88 D2
Harvest Rd SS8 .....168 A6
Harvey Cl SS13 ......121 B1
Harvey Cnr RM20 ....23 D8
Harvey Gdns IG10 ....89 B6
Harvey Ho RM13 .....154 D7
  Ilford RM6 ....134 D7
Harvey Rd Basildon SS13 ..121 C1
  Ilford IG1 ....152 B7

Harvey's La RM7 .....135 E2
Harveyfields RM19 ....65 C5
Harwater Dr IG10 ....88 F7
Harwood Ave RM11 ...136 E8
Harwood Cl RM17 ....178 C8
Harwood Hall La RM14 ..156 B6
Haselfoot Rd CM3 ....33 F8
Haskard Rd RM9 .....153 D7
Haskins SS17 ....144 C4
Haslars Cl CM4 ......74 C4
Haslemere Est The EN11 ..21 C6
Haslemere Pinnacles Est
  The CM19 ....23 A7
Haslemere Rd Ilford IG2 ..133 F2
  Wickford SS12 ......99 C2
Haslewood Ave EN11 ..21 A6
Haslewood Jun Mix Sch
  EN11 ....21 B6
Haslingden Ho **11** RM3 ..114 E5
Hassell Rd SS8 ......164 D3
Hassenbrook Cl SS17 ..160 E1
Hassenbrook Rd SS17 ..160 E1
Hassenbrook Sch SS17 ..160 E2
Hasted Cl CM19 .....22 C2
Hastings Ave IG6 ....133 C7
Hastings Cl RM17 ....177 E8
Hastings Rd Romford RM2 ..136 B6
  Southend-on-S SS1 ..167 B8
Hastings The SS11 ...99 D1
Hastingwood Ct CM5 ..48 F5
Hastingwood Rd
  CM17, CM5 ....24 E4
Hatch Gn CM22 ......2 B8
Hatch Gr RM6 ....134 E7
Hatch La E4 ....109 E7
Hatch Rd CM15 ......94 B4
Hatch Side SS7 ......111 A5
Hatches Farm Rd CM12 ..118 D5
Hatchfields CM3 .....18 F7
Hatchwoods IG8 .....109 F6
Hatfield Cl Brentwood CM15 ..94 D2
  Hornchurch RM12 ....155 D7
  Ilford IG6 ....133 B8
  Redbridge IG6 ......111 B1
Hatfield Dr CM11 ....97 D2
Hatfield Gr CM1 .....31 D1
Hatfield Heath Cty Prim Sch
  CM22 ....3 A3
Hatfield Rd
  Dagenham RM9 ......153 E5
  Heybridge CM9 ......36 B7
  Rayleigh SS6 ....123 B3
Hatfields IG10 ......89 B6
Hathaway Cres E12 ...152 A6
Hathaway Gdns
  Grays RM17 ....173 A3
  Ilford RM6 ....173 B2
Hathaway Rd RM17 ...173 A2
Hatherleigh Way RM3 ..114 D2
Hatherley The SS14 ..142 D7
Hatley Ave IG2 ......133 C7
Hatley Cl SS4 ....144 A5
Hatley Gdns SS4 ....141 D5
Hatterill SS11 ......99 C1
Hatton Cl RM16 .....172 C3
Hatton Sch IG8 .....132 D8
Havana Cl RM1 ......135 C8
Havana Dr SS2 ......123 C7
Havant Ho **El** RM3 ...114 E3
Havelock St IG1 ....163 E3
Haven Cl Basildon SS16 ..142 E3
  Canvey Island SS8 ...163 E3
Haven Pl RM16 ......173 C4
Haven Rd SS8 ....163 D2
Haven Terr RM16 ....119 D6
Haven The RM16 .....173 F2
Havengore Cl SS3 ...150 C3
Havengore Basildon SS13 ..142 E3
  Chelmsford CM5 .....32 F5
Havengore Ho SS9 ...146 E1
Havenside EN9 ......149 E5
Havenwood Cl CM16 ...F H & E
Haverhill Rd E4 ....87 C1
Havering Cl SS3 ....150 B4
Havering Coll of F & H & gnd
  Romford, Ardleigh Green
  RM11 ....136 F3
Havering Cty Prim RM4 ..113 C6
Havering Gdns RM6 ...134 D6
Havering Rd RM11 ...136 D3
Havering Sixth Form Coll
  RM11 ....136 F3
Havering Way IG11 ...153 B2
Havis Rd SS17 ....160 E4
Havisham Way CM1 ...31 E7
Haward Rd EN11 .....21 C8
Hawes La E4 ....65 C1
Hawfinch Wlk CM2 ...54 B5
Hawk Cl EN9 ....66 A5
Hawk Cnr RM20 .....172 D1
Hawk Hill SS11 .....100 D2
Hawk La SS11 ....100 D2
Hawkbush Gn SS13 ...121 B1
Hawkdene E4 ....87 C3
Hawkenbury CM19 ....23 B6
Hawkes Dr CM17 .....178 B8
Hawkesbury Bush La
  SS16 ....142 B2
Hawkesbury Cl SS8 ...163 F2
Hawkesbury Rd SS8 ...163 E2
Hawkhurst Cl RM3 ...114 E3
Hawkhurst Gdns RM5 ..113 B2
Hawkins Gdns IG8 ...105 D5
Hawkinge Gr EN11 ...57 E2
Hawkridge SS13 .....143 B4
Hawkridge Cl RM6 ...134 C5
Hawks Cl CM3 ......57 A6

Hawks Hill CM16 .....47 A4
Hawks La SS5 ....124 E5
Hawksmoor Gn CM13 ..95 D4
Hawksmouth E4 .....87 C2
Hawksway SS10 .....142 B4
Hawkswood Rd CM11 ..99 A6
Hawkwell Chase SS5 ..124 E4
Hawkwell Ct E4 .....109 C2
Hawkwell Ho RM8 ...134 C5
Hawkwell Park Dr SS5 ..125 A5
Hawkwell Park Rd SS5 ..124 F5
Hawkwell Rd SS5 ....124 F6
Hawkwood Cl CM3 ....79 E3
Hawstead IG7 ....88 B2
Hawthorn Ave
  Brentwood CM13 ....116 F6
  Rainham RM13 ......155 B3
Hawthorn Cl
  Chelmsford CM2 .....54 C
  Hockley SS5 ....124 F
Hawthorn Pl DA8 ....169 C
Hawthorn Rd
  Canvey Island SS8 ...164 C
  Hoddesdon EN11 .....21 B
  Woodford IG9 ....110 A8
Hawthorn Way SS6 ...123 F
Hawthorn Wlk CM3 ...79 E
Hawthorne Ct E4 ....109 B
Hawthorne Gdns SS5 ..124 B
Hawthorne Rd SS17 ..160 F
Hawthorns SS0 ....58 D
Hawthorns Harlow CM18 ..23 F
  South Benfleet SS7 ...144 C
  Southend-on-S SS9 ..146 E
  Woodford IG9 ....110 A
Hawthorns The
  Corringham SS17 ....161 C
  Danbury CM3 ....57 F
  Loughton IG10 .....89 F
Hawtree Cl SS1 .....150 A
Hay Cl SS8 ....164 A
Hay Green La CM15 ...72 E
Hay Terr RM20 ......172 C
Hayburn Way RM3 ...135 F
Hayden Cl RM5 ......113 A4
Hayden Way RM5 ....113 A4
Haydens Rd CM20 ....23 D
Haydock Cl RM12 ....155 A
Haydon Rd RM8 .....134 C
Hayes Barton SS1 ...168 C
Hayes Chase SS11 ...101 A
Hayes Cl Chelmsford CM2 ..32 A
  Grays RM20 ....177 A
Hayes Dr RM13 .....155 A
Hayes Hill Farm EN9 ..43 F
Hayes La SS8 ....163 B
Hayes Rd DA9 ....176 A
Haylands Sch CM1 ...31 A
Hayle RM18 ....175 B
Haynes Park Ct RM11 ..136 A
Haynes Rd RM11 ....136 A
Hayrick Cl SS16 ....141 F
Hayron's La High Easter CM1 ..6 A
  Leaden Roding CM1 ...6 A
Haysoms Cl SS1 ....167 B
Haystocks E18 ......132 A
Hayward Sch The CM1 ..32 C
Haywards RM15 .....171 D
Haywards Cl
  Brentwood CM13 ....95 A
  Ilford RM6 ....134 A
Haywood Ct EN9 ....66 A
Hazard Ho DA11 ....179 A
Hazel Cl Basildon SS15 ..179 A
  Hornchurch RM12 ....136 A
  South Benfleet SS7 ...145 A
  Southend-on-S SS9 ..146 A
Hazel Ct **El** Chigwell IG6 ..111 A
  Loughton IG10 .....89 A
Hazel Dr RM15 .....173 A
Hazel Gdns Grays RM16 ..173 A
  Sawbridgeworth CM21 ..1 A
Hazel Gr RM6 ......134 A
Hazel Rise RM11 ...136 A
Hazelbrook Gdns IG6 ..111 A
Hazeldene Rd IG3 ...134 A
Hazeldon Cl CM13 ...19 A
Hazeleigh CM13 ....117 A
Hazeleigh Gdns IG8 ..110 A
Hazeleigh Hall La CM3 ..58 A
Hazell Cres RM5 ...113 A
Hazelmere SS6 ....146 A
Hazelmere Gdns RM11 ..136 A
Hazelwood Hockley SS5 ..124 A
  Loughton IG10 .....88 A
Hazelwood Cres SS5 ..124 A
Hazelwood Ct CM9 ...37 A
Hazelwood Gr SS9 ...124 A
Hazelwood Park Cl **5**
  IG7 ....111 A
Hazlemere Rd SS4 ...58 A
Head St CM7 ....38 A
Headcorn Cl SS13 ...
Headingham Ho SS6 ..123 A
Headingley Cl IG6 ...133 A
Headley App IG2 ....113 A
Headley Cl IG2 ....133 A
Headley Chase CM14 ..137 A
Headley Dr IG2 ....133 A
Headley Rd CM11 ...97 A
Heard's La CM15 ...73 A
Hearn Rd RM11 ....139 A
Hearsall Ave
  Chelmsford CM1 ....
  Stanford-le-H SS17 ..160 A
Heath Cl Billericay CM12 ..96 A
  Romford RM2 ....
Heath Dr Chelmsford CM2 ..